How to ROCK at BJD Face-Up

A Beginner's Guide to Painting Resin Doll Faces

By

Jesslyn Carver

How to Rock at BJD Face-Up: A Beginner's Guide to Painting Resin Doll Faces

Copyright 2014 Jesslyn Carver

ISBN: 978-0-9982104-0-7 (paperback)

ISBN: 978-0-9982104-1-4 (ebook)

Dorwik Publishing

Greenbrier, TN

Table of Contents

Foreword

Welcome to the BJD hobby! Your pursuit of a new skill in this wonderful and strange new art form is an admirable undertaking. It takes a little money, practice, and imagination but you are about to tap into a new creative world with boundless possibilities for expression.

I decided to become a Ball-Jointed Doll collector and face-up artist in 2012. I had, of course, seen photos of these otherworldly little people first and went through a few emotional stages before finally coming out as an actual owner of one. First there was amazement and longing for such a bizarrely beautiful object, every one of which seemed to have life inside of it somehow. Then my little buzz was killed when I noticed that I could not afford one. I was thrown into a darker stage when it looked like I would have to spend hundreds of dollars to hire someone to paint my doll's face. They would be using super expensive airbrush equipment that I had no idea about and wasn't really interested in dishing out the money and discipline to learn (airbrush had always been a little too high-tech for this old-fashioned, hand-painting girl). I don't remember whose blog I was reading at that time, but thinking back on it now makes me laugh.

Roll the calendar forward about five or ten more years and I'm in my twenties, married, and making my own money. I rediscovered Asian Ball-Jointed dolls (or BJD's as we lovingly call them) and noticed a new company that may not have been around when I was a teen. It was called Resin Soul, based in South Korea. These dolls were not only beautiful to me and came with awesome pointy ears that I've always wanted in a doll, but they were incredibly affordable. I decided to go all the way and get a $200 elf-boy named Long. That price was pushing it for me, but I decided that that was what I was getting. As I saved my money I did extensive internet research to learn everything I could about this hobby. It changed my life when I heard about the technique for using soft pastels with a spray sealant to get the same softly blushed appearance that can be achieved with an airbrush. From this point, I knew everything was going to be all right as far as giving a personality to my new beloved resin boy.

My very first face-up allowed me to get a feel for the process. It was NOT one that I kept. It was done on a large "soft resin" Obitsu head that cost me about $20. I did two face-ups on the Obitsu head and when my Resin Soul arrived in the mail, it took two tries again before I was happy with the result. Art is not about following someone's exact instructions, doing as they do, and then having a perfect work of art on the first try. First I would say it's about love and passion: you should love what you are doing, the process and the result, and you should have a burning passion driving you forward.

It's safe to say that I don't paint because I want to—it's because I have to. If you are un-sure about starting this endeavor, you may want to start by asking yourself, "Why do I want to do this?" If you are also wondering whether you should even buy a doll, your an-swers to the above question may be helpful. This is an expensive hobby and should not be taken lightly. On the other hand, I believe that art is about the five stages of the Creative Process, which are preparation, frustration, incubation, illumination, and revision. Let's put an emphasis on "frustration." That's right. We all have that—especially the profession-als! So you should get used to it. The good news is that there are three great stages that follow. Incubation time happens when you take a break from the project. It gives your brain time to mull over the project whether you're consciously thinking about it or not. Even while you sleep your brain is trying to solve your problems for you! Illumination happens in that magic moment when you finally understand or come up with the solution to the problem. And then revision is the part where you get back into the project, do some more work, and step back to see how it looks. This may be the finishing step or you may experience more frustration and do the steps all over again. Eventually you'll get comfort-able and learn to decide for yourself what works for you and how to achieve the look you want. No two artists do or should have to follow the exact same process!

It's good to ask other artists for constructive criticism if you feel you need help, but don't let anyone tell you that your face-up is wrong or bad. No face up is wrong. There are some who did the face-up purposefully and there are some who just need a little practice. If you sense someone being malicious online, it's best to cut the conversation there. There may be slight competition in the BJD hobby if you choose to enter one at a convention or doll meet, but otherwise, it's not about that at all. In reality it's you and your doll. No one else matters after that. Remember, art is an extremely subjective thing just as jealousy and negativity are extremely destructive things.

I am here to give you all the technical aspects of the art of face-up. I can tell you what supplies you need and how they work together. When it comes to the actual creative part, like choosing colors, please feel free to branch off and try anything that takes your fancy! By all means, you are welcome to copy my face-ups—I am not threatened by this—but I think what you really would appreciate is designing your own unique style and char-acter.

The bad news is this process is not cheap. I spent $50+ alone on pastels. And even when you try to cut corners, the prices still seem to add up in the long run. Expense is one of the joys of being an artist and I accepted that a long time ago. If this puts you off, you may decide not to do this yourself, and that's ok. There are many artists online who have competitive prices—perhaps as low as $50.

The difference is that when you have the tools, they last quite a long time and you can continue to repaint your doll's face, future doll faces, or even make money by becoming a face-up artist-for-hire yourself. Let's say you tried doing a face-up and decided you don't like it, it's not fun—it's frustrating, or you're happy with your doll now and have no plans to do another one. But you spent all that money! Some other good news is that you may be able to get most of it back by selling the whole lot on eBay or Etsy under the label of being a "BJD Face-Up Kit." You might get half or most of your money back and you'll be helping someone else out who is struggling with wrangling up the supplies needed. The choice is yours! The best news is:

This is the easiest art form I've ever tried.

Yes, go back and savor that last sentence if you want. I use and have tried many different art forms in my chosen art career, (oil painting especially) and it's true. Pastels are extremely light and forgiving and easy to erase. Having said that, if you decide that you hate paint and watercolor pencils, you can choose to do your face-up using only pastels and it can still look great! If you hate the face-up you made, never fear, just wipe it off with the brush cleaner, give it a little dish detergent bath, and try again tomorrow. If I made an oil painting and at the end decided I hated it, guess what, the art store doesn't give refunds for canvases that have been painted on. However much money I spent on that canvas is gone. And oil paint is permanent and hard to paint over. But a resin (and also plastic or vinyl) doll head can ALWAYS be cleaned off and repainted—weather you hated the first try or if you've enjoyed the face-up for years and decided that you want to try something new for a change.

Raivo (my Resin Soul "Long") has been wearing his face-up for about two years. He just got a new wig and it doesn't look right with that old face-up. So I think he could use an update. Come watch as he gets his new face on!

Chapter 1

Tools of the Trade

Here is a list of tools and mediums you will need. Some are optional and will be listed under the "Optional" heading. This is what I best recommend. There are alternatives if you wish to try something different. But this is the list that I use and the only supplies I can truthfully recommend based on my experience.

Mediums

1.Mister Super Clear (MSC) Sealant: This is a sealant spray can. Make sure you get the one that says "matt" or "flat" in English on the can. If you get the one labeled "gloss," then you can expect a very shiny doll. I will go ahead and recommend this above any other sealants in question. You can try other sealants if you wish, but this is what I know will work and is used by most other face-up artists. It is a Japanese product with all directions in Japanese. I will explain how to use it in Chapter 3. It works, it's removable, and it really is "super clear." The only downside to this product is that if you are in the USA or any other non-Asian country, you will probably have to order it online. It also never hurts to ask your local craft store if they can order it for you. I usually get mine on eBay from China for about fifteen dollars. The further downside to ordering it from China or other Asian countries is that they have to ship it by sea mail, which takes at least two months to get to my house. Just be patient and make sure you know how long it will take. Eventually, it will get to you (unless the post office loses it, but isn't that a risk we all take when we order stuff?).

The other places to order it, that I would recommend, are the websites JunkySpot.com, which specializes in all things BJD, and Amazon.com.

Alternative Sealants

I've heard that it can be hard or even impossible to get Mister Super Clear in some European countries. But fear not, friends, because there are European and worldwide alternatives that work just as well. Here are two alternative sealants that are reported to work and remove. But keep in mind that different people have had different experiences and opinions about these alternatives. These two have been reported to work, but none I've ever heard of is as widely accepted as MSC. Please try these at your own risk.

Lukas Acrylic Medium Spray Film: A European product. Recommended for Resin only. Has been reported to produce varied negative effects on vinyl and plastic, but seems to work well on resin. Can be layered several times, is protective, and non-yellowing. Available locally in certain European countries and also found on Amazon.com for the rest of the world.

Citadel Purity Seal: This one was made specifically for painting gaming miniatures which is very similar to what we are doing. It is an American product and the can is in English. The can advertises a satin finish, but they say it is matte enough for a face-up. I've heard it is available worldwide.

2.Soft Pastels or Nupastels: Soft pastels are dry chalky sticks of color. They should be available anywhere art supplies are sold and there are a variety of set sizes. Avoid the type called "oil pastels." Soft Pastels and Nupastels are basically the same. The only difference is that Nupastels are compatible with water and can be used as a watercolor cake for painting. I use the brands Prismacolor and Gallery, but you can probably get away with using any brand you want as long as it is called "soft" and not "oil."

3.Acrylic Paint: Avoid oil-based paints. They will not work. You can use acrylic, watercolor, or gouache, as long as it is water-based. Acrylic is the most commonly used for this. It is versatile and can be watered down to any consistency you want. Acrylic is basically a liquid plastic and dries tough, flexible, and waterproof. It is what I use, so I'm going to refer to it throughout this book.

Two of the best brands are Liquitex and a slightly cheaper brand called Master's Touch. They look identical to me once they are on the palette. Though all acrylic brands, cheap and pricy, are compatible to use together, so mix them up as you please. You can start with any colors you want but I will go ahead and recommend these to start your palette for a good range of color mixing: Cadmium Red, Alizarin Crimson, Cadmium Yellow, Ultramarine Blue, Titanium White, and Raw Umber. If you want to go ahead and buy more than that then you can add these for an even broader range: Burnt Umber, Burnt Sienna, Lemon Yellow, Yellow Ochre, Cobalt Blue, and Cerulean Blue. Notice that I did not mention black! I'll tell you why in Chapter 6.

> *Note: though they are both acrylic, "artist paint" is recommended over "craft paint." Craft paint is tempting because it costs a fraction of what artist paint costs. But overall, artist paint is better quality. You get what you pay for in this industry.*

4.Acrylic Paint Thinner: Yes you can get away with using water. But remember that acrylic dries fast and water makes it dry faster. Unless you love the "dry brush" technique, you might want to enhance your water with an acrylic thinner. I use Liquitex Flow-Aid. It is the only acrylic thinner I've used and can't recommend any other brands. But you're welcome to experiment—as long as it thins acrylic you can't go wrong. One bottle of Flow Aid will probably last your whole life because you're actually supposed to mix it with water. I do this in a little squirt bottle so I can dispense one drop at a time onto the palette. It takes 1 part Flow-Aid to 20 parts water. I used a half-teaspoon measurement to do this. It slows drying time (which is actually a good thing) and increases the flow and workability of the paint.

5.Watercolor Pencils: This can either be used alongside the paint or you can skip the paint and use these instead. Some people are more comfortable with a pencil than a brush, and that's understandable. I have and use both. Even if you want to use the brush, the pencils may still come in handy. For instance if you want to draw a detailed tattoo on your doll, you could use a light-colored pencil (like yellow) to draw the basic design guidelines and cover them with your paint strokes (making sure to seal in between these two elements because the watery paint will make the pencil line run). Make sure you get watercolor pencils and not regular colored pencils. Watercolor pencils are designed to dissolve and run on contact with water. This makes them easy to use and remove from the doll head. The "leads" may also be softer than regular colored pencils and can therefore mark the sealant-covered resin much better.

6. Acrylic Gloss: This is what you will use to put a shiny coat on the lips and/or eyes of your doll to make them look moist. As long as it is considered for acrylic paint and therefore water-based, it is pretty easy to choose a gloss. I would get an acrylic varnish, which is a glaze used to cover the finished painting in order to protect it. Don't bother buying "matte" because that's the same as "flat," it will not shine and there is no point in using it on your doll. I particularly use Liquitex Gloss Varnish. It has proven to work for me and remove. just fine. With this particular varnish, it may not be very shiny with just one coat. I like this because it is controllable. I can use one coat for a boy's lips, making them shiny enough to look moist, and for a girl's lips I can add multiple coats, letting each dry before applying the next, to make it look like she is wearing shiny lip gloss. When it comes to choosing a brand of gloss, read the directions and make sure it is water-based to see if it will work. As long as it says "gloss" it will dry shiny and you can probably use it.

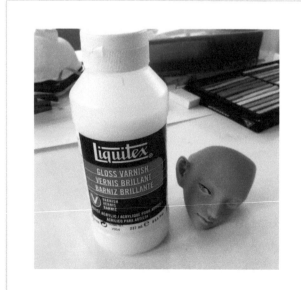

Tools

1. Mask: This one is the most important! The sealant is very toxic and should be sprayed outside while wearing a mask to prevent inhalation. I will talk more about this in Chapter 3. At the very least you should get a good thick dust mask with a respirator filter.

The best idea is to buy a large one with the two big filters. People always ask if they can just hold their breath while spraying. The answer is NO. Just buy a mask. Painting a doll is not worth the damage inhaling the sealant will do to your body. Even when I'm wearing mine, I still breathe shallowly and turn my face away from the spray mist.

2. Brushes: When it comes to shape and size this can be entirely up to you. Just remember to get ones with synthetic bristles because the natural hog hair brush is too stiff and coarse for what we want to do. You'll need short-handled brushes--the long-handled ones are used for oil painting. The synthetic brushes look soft and silky and can come in any color in the world. I like to use mainly small flat brushes (they have rectangular-shaped bristles) around size 6 or 8. You should have a variety of shapes and sizes to discover what you find most helpful and for the freedom of creativity. There is no science to

finding the perfect brush and this can be one of the cheapest supplies you buy (variety sets are recommended). Some people like to use angled flat brushes for shaping eyebrows. You'll have to decide if you want to do this or not. For fine lines like eyelashes, you'll want to find the tiniest round brush possible. The smallest size I can find is called 20/0 and I've also seen 10/0 and 12/0. Bristle length might play a major part here: longer bristles hold more paint and shorter gives you more control. I prefer short-little-barely-there bristles. But you should try both and see what you like. You should also pick a large brush as your "sweeper." This can be as large or small as you want but I recommend softer bristles. You will use it

to sweep away excess pastel dust from the doll's face, but you don't want it to erase the color entirely.

3. Erasers: Not only are they used to correct mistakes, but they are also a valuable drawing tool. You'll need a kneaded eraser which is grey and soft. It looks like clay and you can mold it into any shape you need. And kneading it with your hands, stretching it out, and squishing it back together will clean the surface! You can use it to soften your pastel work as well as reshape it. The other type is the white plastic eraser. Just as it sounds, it's white and usually rectangular. As it's harder than the kneaded eraser, it will hold its shape and "cut" sharp lines through pastel marks.

4. Gloves: Latex rubber, vinyl, or cotton, the choice is yours. I can find latex and vinyl easier in stores. Obviously cotton is more breathable and you can keep it a little longer because you can wash it. This and vinyl are also the obvious choice for people who are allergic to latex rubber. A box of one hundred rubber gloves lasts me a long time because I only use one on the hand that holds the doll's head while I'm working. Make sure to use a fresh one every time to avoid marking up the doll's head passively with old pastel stains.

5. Craft Knife: This is a pencil-like handle with interchangeable razor blades for precision cutting. It is useful for a variety of oddball jobs, particularly shaving pastel powder off the stick and slicing wedges off your white plastic eraser.

6. Paint Mixing / Palette Knife: I recommend one for your acrylic mixing. You might be tempted to buy a cheap plastic knife-thing located near the mixing knives, but don't give in. Just get a good one made of metal with a wooden handle if you're going to be mixing acrylic paint for this hobby. The metal one is more precise and can scoop and scrape and move that paint around on the palette like a pro.

7. Palette for Paint-Mixing: This is a surface for mixing your paint. You have a variety of options. I've known people to mix their acrylic paint on a porcelain dinner plate, wash it off when done, and then return it to the cupboard. You can use this but it might be a better idea in general to use an old plate that is no longer in service. If there are no old plates ready to retire in your home then you could try Goodwill or yard sales and probably get all you need for practically nothing. There are also disposable palette pads with about ten tear-off sheets available in the art stores which are convenient for cleanup. But my favorite palette of all, if you're serious about painting, is a glass palette! It can be found on the web, such as eBay, online art stores, and sometimes local art stores. It's shaped like a traditional artist palette and cleans up nicely because you can abandon the paint to let dry and then use a razor blade paint scraper to remove the dried paint later. If you want to clean up immediately while the paint is still wet, you can wash it in the kitchen sink with water if you're using water-based paint (this is how you would also clean the dinner plate palette). The glass palette is pricy, but worth it if you are seriously considering painting or face-up as a permanent hobby.

Note: if you use a dinner plate for mixing paint, it's best to get a solid white or tan color for this job. Avoid confusing high-detail decorative designs.

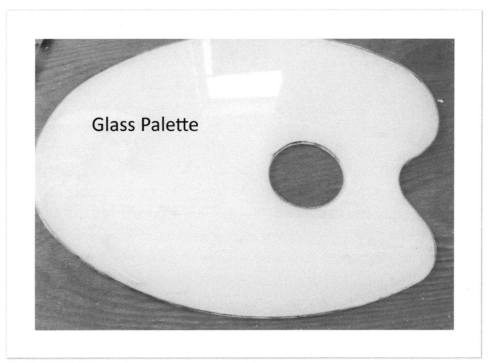

Glass Palette

8. Palette for Pastels: You need a place to drop and mix those pastel powders, of course. Some people just use a sheet of notebook paper. This or a paper plate apparently works but keep in mind that the pastel may bond to the paper product and thus you will lose some. The more powder you can salvage, the longer you can keep working. Another option is a Styrofoam plate which shouldn't absorb any powder. I personally used that old retired dinner plate idea for my pastels. No complaints. It's plain white and I just blow the old powder out the door when my colors need refreshing. For pastel palettes you can think outside the box—no need to spend a bunch of money at the craft store on this one!

9. Pencil Sharpener: You'll need this to sharpen your watercolor pencils, but don't spend a bunch of money on something fancy. You just need that little blade to be sharp! So buy non-fancy and as cheap as possible. After a while you'll need to replace it because the blade will get dull. Your watercolor pencils are expensive, so take care of them by replacing the sharpener often. After sharpening the pencil as well as it can manage, you may need to use the craft knife to improve the fine point. Just graze the knife along the colored lead very gently and you might obtain a more perfect precision point for those tiny eyelash lines.

10. Magic Eraser: It's like a white sponge you use to clean any surface. They are ideal for cleaning resin dolls. Not only can you use it to clean odd marks and smudges off the doll as everyday maintenance, you can also use it to scrub off the previous face-up. I recommend cutting off little squares and wedges any time you need to use it, instead of using the whole thing. It will last a very long time if you do this. Both name brand and generic work the same.

Warning: The Magic Eraser is useful but powerful! It acts sort of like sandpaper and can actually sand the resin down gradually. This may be the gentlest way to sand the seams off your doll if it needs it. But if you are buffing off the old sealant and pastel then be very gentle and do not rub vigorously in concentrated areas. It just may rub off your dolls abs or nipples! I discovered this on my own when I was cleaning off my tan-colored doll's torso and noticed the new pale area where I had been scrubbing fast and hard; it had taken off a fraction of the resin's surface and exposed newer resin underneath. No harm was done to the sculpting, but now I know to go slower next time and probably do my vigorous scrubbing with a cotton swab or pad instead. In this hobby it's always a good idea to take your time.

11. Winsor & Newton Brush Cleaner and Restorer: I'm telling you the exact brand to get, because I know this one will work and many people use it. It's made for cleaning paint brushes for both water and oil paints. It removes paint residue that has long dried and will therefore remove all the paint, sealant, and gloss from an existing face-up. It's strong stuff but is basically harmless. It's ok to get it on your hands, but you will want to wash them well when you're finished. I have been asked if we need to wear a mask while using it. I don't think so. It's claimed to be non-toxic on the bottle and smells just like nail polish remover. Some people actually use nail polish remover and if you choose this option it's best to choose a colorless brand. Some people prefer the acetone-free type.

> Warning: Just like the magic eraser, brush cleaner is also useful but powerful. It tends to soften the resin and make it more susceptible to scratches (but this is not a permanent effect). If you are using a needle or other metal tool to clean your doll alongside brush cleaner, take extreme care. And whatever you do, do NOT soak a resin doll part in a bowl of acetone, acetone-free nail polish remover, or brush cleaner for any amount of time. It has been reported to ruin the item and release fumes that may damage your health!

12: A Small Squirt Bottle: This is for mixing your acrylic thinner with water (if the instructions on your thinner says to do that) and dispensing your thinner. Get one with a long nozzle that allows one drop out at a time, this will make it easy to add thinner to the paint on your palette. I got mine from the painting section in my local craft store.

13: Odds and Ends: The magic eraser may count as one of these but it's such a special item that I gave it its own place on the list. Here are some odds and ends I suggest you have with you at all times for painting and removing face-ups: Paper towels, cotton swabs, cotton pads, toothpicks, plastic cup, and a sewing needle.

Optional

1: Apron: With all that paint and sealant, face-up work can be a messy job. If you don't have or want one, you can wear old clothes. I have not noticed anything about MSC to be harmful to my clothes, but I like having an apron to wipe my hands on while painting. Another option, if you are serious about art, is a snazzy pair of scrubs. I recently decided to make scrubs my proud artist's uniform. And I say let the paint splash!

2: Work Glasses/Goggles: I don't wear these, but you can feel free if you are worried about getting the sealant mist in your eyes.

3: Pearl Ex Pigments: This is an optional effect element in the form of dry powder. There are several different colors, one of which is a silver glitter you can use to add a little sparkle to your face-up. Just dust it on with a brush and then you have to seal it in place with the sealant—just like pastel powder.

4: Acetone: This can be used to remove 3D eyelashes from your doll. Nail polish remover may be used instead as it often contains acetone. Some people also use nail polish remover instead of Brush Cleaner to remove a face-up. Note: if you have the earlier-mentioned brush cleaner, that will also work to remove glue so you can skip the acetone.

5: Liquitex puts out a large variety of additional products for cool effects. They have an iridescent paint medium which interests me. And don't forget about neon and glow in the dark colors! As long as it's acrylic, it's useable.

6: Ribbon: For detaching the doll head from its body.

Ok you've got all the stuff listed above. And you have a doll head with a face-up that needs removing. If not then just give the head a little wash in warm water with dish detergent (to remove any dirt or hard-to-see oily fingerprints), let air dry for a few hours, and skip the next chapter. Now I'm going to remove Raivo's face!

"Don't worry, Raivo, this won't hurt."

Chapter 2

A Doll's Rebirth: Removing the Old Face-up

Detaching the Doll's Head

It is very much recommended to remove the doll's head for this whole process. Don't worry, the doll won't mind. This may feel uncomfortable to first-timers, it was for me, but give it a try and then you will be empowered to attach and detach as many times as needed and for whatever reason.

All you will need is a ribbon and a pair of knees, or in some cases a partner to hold the doll's body steady while you do the muscle work.

First remove the doll's head cap or faceplate, which should be held in place by pegs or magnets. Certain dolls with pegs may require you to wedge your fingernails, or other flat object, gently into the crease and work the two pieces apart. Please go slow and do not use excessive force.

On the inside you should see the neck opening with an S-hook, metal ring, or a turn-key system made from resin. If your doll has the turn-key system then simply twist the "key" part so that it aligns with the slot and then lift the doll head off of the neck.

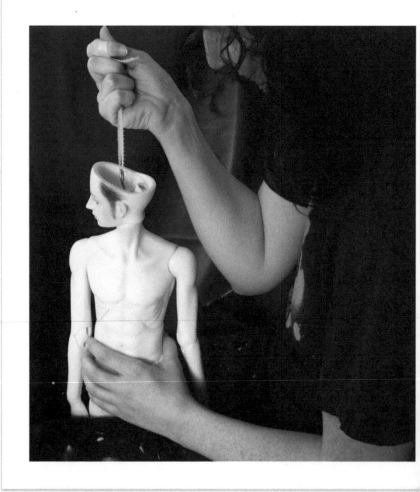

For a ring or S-hook you will need to insert the ribbon through the hook, pull it upward, stretching the doll's elastic string (remembering to brace the doll between your knees), and then twist the hook/ring or dolls head so that the hook/ring aligns parallel to the neck opening slot and then ease the elastic back down to rest. The metal hook/ring should now be sitting down below the ground of the inner doll head, and you can lift the head off the neck. The hook/ring should now be sitting atop the doll's neck, holding the string and the whole doll together.

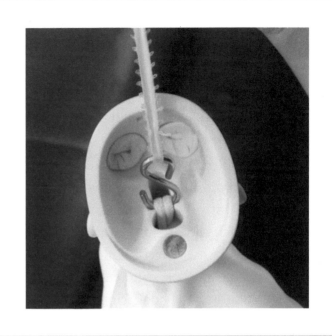

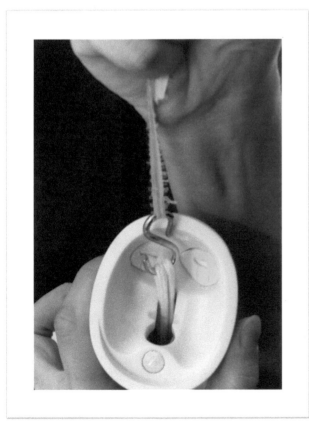

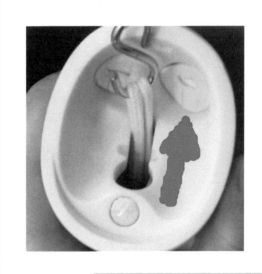

Settle the hook parallel with the neck opening.

Reattaching the Doll's Head

To reattach the head, reverse the steps for re-moving it. First, thread the ribbon through the hook/ring and then thread its two ends through the opening in the doll head. The head should now be resting on the neck and over the hook/ring. The next step will require a bit of muscle. With the doll braced between your knees or held steady by a partner, pull on the ribbon to lift the hook/ring through the head opening. Rotate the hook or doll head so that the hook/ring lands perpendicular to the open-ing slit. Make sure the hook/ring settles into the groove that is usually present, running across the opening slit. Now you can remove the ribbon and replace the head cap.

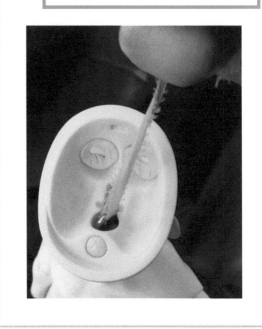

This head is unlocked and ready For removal.

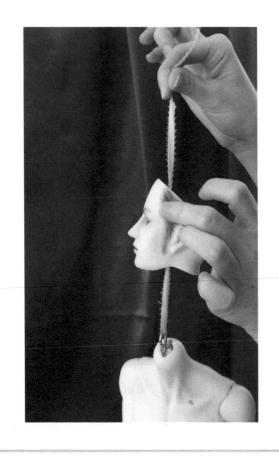

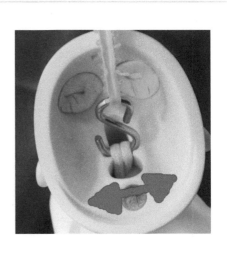

Settle the hook perpendicular with the neck opening and then the head is secure and ready for dress-up!

Removing the Old Face up

Supplies Needed: Doll head, Brush Cleaner, Magic Eraser, toothpicks, cotton pads, cotton swabs, paper towel, plastic table cover, scrap paper, rubber gloves (optional).

First you'll need to set up your work station. I work at a desk where it's ok to spill paint and stuff here and there. If you only have your mom's antique dining table at which to work, you should do her and yourself a favor by protecting it first. Some sort of plastic tarp or table cloth to cover the good table would be ideal. I like to set up a sort of place mat for both removal and face-up work with a large-size scrap paper that's clean and I can rest my doll head on and also use a corner to make practice marks. Cotton pads soaked in brush cleaner can be messy and will bleed through the paper, which is why it's good to have plastic underneath. Make sure your surface is cleaned and restored before moving on to the face-up process! I don't recommend newspaper because I can foresee the print rubbing off on the doll's head as it does our fingers. If nothing else, I would spread a few sheets of clean typing paper on my work surface. This may be a good way to recycle scrap documents (old school papers etc.) as long as they are neat and their back sides are unprinted.

Right on your paper place mat (if you have one) spread your tools around. Place your bottle of Brush Cleaner, cotton pads, a paper towel, toothpicks, cotton swabs, a sewing needle, and a square or two of Magic Eraser. Set everything where you can reach them comfortably.

Did your doll come with 3D eyelashes? If so you'll have to peel them away carefully with a fine pair of tweezers. Hopefully the glue will come with them, but if not then you may be able to peel the rest of it away with the tweezers. If the glue is too stubborn, apply a little brush cleaner with a cotton swab. The brush cleaner, and alternative nail polish remover, contains acetone which can remove the glue. Once they are wet down, the eyelashes should peel away more easily. Use it as neatly and sparingly as possible and be sure to wash the doll head when you are finished if you don't plan to remove the rest of the face-up immediately.

First, I would grab a cotton pad, use it to plug the opened bottle of brush cleaner, and give it a little dip to moisten the cotton. Now start rubbing at the face-up and watch it slowly disappear. When you find places that are more stubborn, you can switch to a square of Magic Eraser to buff the paint off a little more easily.

A cotton pad can be used to wipe off most of the face-up.

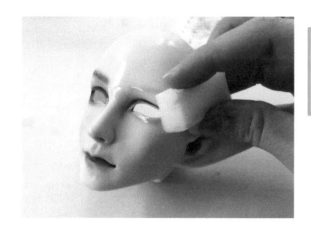

A square clipped off a magic eraser can be used to buff off stubborn marks.

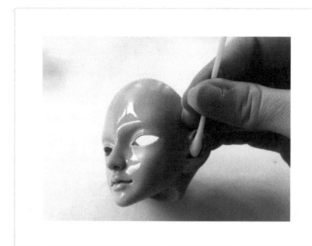

Depending on the size of the doll head, you can dip a cotton swab into the Brush cleaner and then start working on the eyeholes to remove the darkened edges. And if it will fit, you may be able to stick the cotton swab into the nostrils to remove any shading that might be in there. For smaller dolls, you can use a toothpick to gently scratch the paint out of the nostrils and corners of the eyes.

You will also use the toothpick to painstakingly rub the shading from between the lips. This is the worst part in my opinion. My Resin Soul dolls have deeply sculpted lip creases and it is a pain to get all that paint out of there. This part may take the longest, but just hang in there. The longer you work, the better result you'll see. Don't forget to work on the ears. For the small spaces, it often works well to drape the soaked cotton pad over a toothpick and stick it into the nostrils, ears, and eyes for a thin handy scrubbing tool. Do a few good rounds around the entire head, wherever it looks like there is sealant and color remaining, and when you think you can't get any more out you might be done.

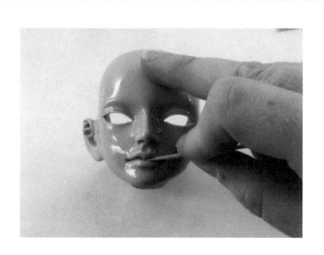

The object is to completely remove every bit of color so that you are left with as pure a piece of resin as possible. Before stopping, make sure that all possible "gunk" is out of the lip crease as well as splinters from the toothpicks—which can sometimes be left behind. But fear not—if you have a sewing needle handy, you can very carefully use this to pick out those splinters. It may also get any remaining color still left behind but be very careful.

Warning: Some people use a sewing needle to scrape the paint and sealant from between the lips. But be careful because the resin is softened by the brush cleaner and if you see "gunk" still coming out after a long while, it might just be resin dust scraped away by the sharp metal needle! Using a toothpick for this job might be a safer method. You should also take your time. Instead of furiously scraping away to try to get all the sealant and paint off on the first round, it may be better to take a break, wash the head and let dry, and then inspect the dried head to see what you missed. Then you can return to the cleaning process again if need be.

The old pastel and paint melts away fairly easily when brush cleaner is used.

Now we'll give the head a final wash. You can draw him, or her, a nice bath in a bowl from the kitchen filled with warm water and dish detergent. I do this process in the sink to stay tidy. You can use your bare hands or a soft cloth to rotate the head around underwater and rub at it. This doesn't have to take very long. Afterward, you can rinse it under the faucet and then place it on a towel to air dry. Your doll head should look beautiful and clean with minimal to no color remaining. I like to clean my doll heads on the day before painting, so it can dry overnight.

> Warning: Letting the head air dry is recommended, but please do NOT place the resin object in direct sunlight to dry. Sunlight speeds up the aging/yellowing process of the resin.

Once it's dry, look it over for crusty or filmy residue before proceeding to the next step. During cleaning, it is usually hard to tell if we removed all the sealant. If you see a little residue, a magic eraser might be able to take care of it. But if you see a lot of residue, give it another wipe-down with brush cleaner, wash, rinse, let dry, and repeat as needed until your doll head looks perfect and new.

Now as soon as this head is dry and we have nice day, we'll start our face-up!

Chapter 3

It's a Lovely Day for a Face-up!

How does the weather look today? Is it nice and sunny? Is it windy? How windy? Is there any humidity? Or is it too cold? Is it...raining?

Why ask? Because all of these things can effect or ruin the face-up. Ideally, we want to wait for a beautiful day with little or no wind, no rain, no humidity, and no extreme temperature. When I did my first face-up on an Obitsu head, it was during a scorching summer. I wasn't sure if it came out quite right when I saw the Mister Super Clear sealant had a "frosted" texture. That's who we're trying to please. Mister Super Clear is a very sensitive dude. But I tried again the next time at night when there was less humidity. Since then I have managed to get my face-ups done during some bizarre seasons. If it's winter time and really cold at night but moderate during the day, this may be the time to work. If we're having a really hot summer, we probably want to try working at night. If it is raining, snowing, or high wind—forget it. On the other hand, if your sealant coat still looks odd, see how far away you are holding it from the can. It has to be at a good distance—not too close.

With practice, you'll learn to judge when it's a good time to do a face-up and when not. If you do happen to mess up a face-up, due to weather or holding the can too close, never fear. Just pull your removal stuff back out and start again. Even when I have no dolls to paint, I still find myself examining the weather and saying, "It's a lovely day for a face-up!"

Sealant: Why all the Trouble?

It's super important! First you need a base coat of sealant on the resin. Think of a house painter who uses a coat of primer before he actually paints the walls, or an oil painter who uses a few coats of gesso on her canvas so the oil paint doesn't eat right through the canvas over time.

Sealant protects the resin from those mean paints who might want to stain it. Particularly intense colors (like red) just might do that. With a good coat of sealant, the colors are not even touching the resin. It will not become stained and will be easier to remove later.

The sealant also adds what we call "tooth" for the pastel powder to grab onto. Otherwise it will slide right off the resin's smooth surface. You have to prepare your canvas before you start the masterpiece.

The good news is that it only takes a minute or two for the sealant to dry. In fact, I never really have to wait more than two minutes before jumping into the pastel phase. There is no exact amount of time I can tell you to wait. I always just watch for the wet shine to disappear. Mister Super Clear "Flat" is not supposed to be shiny. Once it dries, you won't even see it—you'll only know it's there by the new texture the resin will have. That's right. Expect your doll's face to feel a little bit rougher now. This is that "tooth" I was telling you about. I can't confirm what other brand sealants are supposed to feel or look like because I've only used MSC.

How to Seal

Supplies Needed: Doll head, Sealant can, Mask, Glove, Apron and Goggles (optional).

Safety

Put a glove on the hand that will be holding the doll head. Put your mask on, grab your doll head and your can of sealant and let's go outside!

Do I have to go outside? YES.

Do I have to wear a mask? YES!

It's just better for your health and the health of those around you to not spray the sealant in your breathing space. Sealant is an unnatural, manmade chemical that dries and hardens. You don't want it in your lungs. Don't make me have to do a full-length, scientific, explanation as to why you shouldn't breathe it—that would be boring and take up space I could be using to talk about this wonderful art. So spray it outside, wear a mask, don't breathe it. It will damage your lungs, brain, and/or kill you. Consider yourself warned.

But don't be afraid to use it now either. Just be responsible and respect this tool. You're an artist now!

Once you're outside, you'll want to pay attention to the wind direction. If you spray against the wind, the mist will either blow into your face or will be snatched away and none will land on your doll.

Note: I do not wear any work goggles for this job because as I calculate the wind direction I can keep the sealant mist out of my eyes. But if you are nervous about this then please don't hesitate to get yourself a pair. And don't worry about looking silly in front of the neighbors—you're an artist now!

If you are using Mister Super Clear, like I am, you'll notice all the writing on the can, including directions, are in Japanese. I can't read that, but never fear, because all sealant cans should have just about the same safety instructions and we can still learn to use this one safely.

Here is the gist of the Safety Instructions as they appear on a similar domestic can of sealant: Like any other aerosol can, you should keep it out of extreme temperatures. Don't smoke while using it or have any other sort of open flame. Keep it in a safe place so the can cannot get punctured accidentally, and do not throw the empty can into a trash compactor. Spray it outside! Also keep away from Children! Don't spray it around unmasked children even if you are outside! Don't spray around pets either—especially birds. If it gets into your eyes, flush thoroughly with water for 15 minutes and get medical attention. If it gets on your skin wash thoroughly with soap and water. If you experience headache and/or dizziness immediately seek fresh air and if you have trouble breathing, call a physician. Remember, always respect your tools!

Spraying

Mask, glove, and optional goggles on? Good. Let's spray that head! Don't be nervous. Just hold both items at arm's length away and point it so that the can will spray away from your face. Turn yourself in the direction the wind is blowing. Hold the head about 18 inches (46 cm) away from the can and start spraying. Try not to hold the head too close or it may alter the texture in a bad way. Remember, the coat has to be invisible once dry. Rotate the head around in the soft cloud of mist, letting each side get its fair share. I never bother with the back of the head, but unless you feel it needs protecting or if you want to paint a hairline or tattoo back there, then don't forget to turn it around and spray there. When you feel the head has been sprayed thoroughly, you can go ahead and take it back inside to dry. Hold the object by its edges and avoid touching or smearing across the wet surface! Just place it on your work table and give it a minute. So right after you have stripped and washed the head and allowed to air dry, it should now be wearing a generous coat of fresh sealant. As soon as it doesn't look wet anymore, you can apply the first coat of pastel!

Chapter 4

Color Theory

Say hello to the Color Wheel! An artist's best friend. It's full of neat tricks. You can refer back to this image any time you're wondering how to achieve certain colors. I'm going to tell you a little about this tool before we jump right in to using color. Forgive me if I get a little technical, but I don't intend to teach you cheap how-to tricks. I want you to know, not only how to do something, but why you are doing it. This way, you can make your own judgments and know how to achieve your unique goal in future projects. So let's get to it!

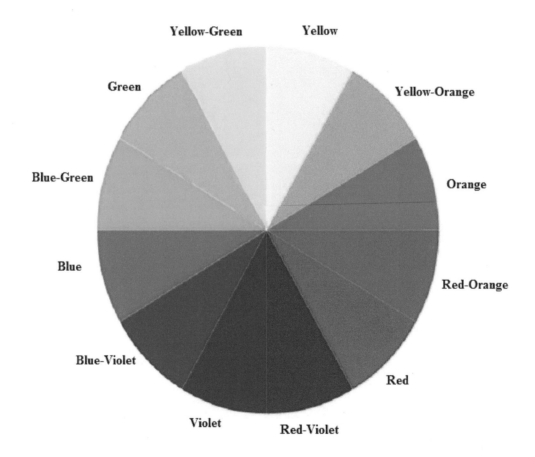

On the color wheel, you can locate the three Primary Colors. They are red, yellow, and blue. These colors are used to mix the Secondary Colors located between them: purple, green, and orange. Between those you can see the six Tertiary Colors which are hyphenated (red-orange, blue-green, etc.). White is usually located in the center because it is a mixture of the whole color spectrum. If ever there is a question of how to mix these colors then you can refer back to the color wheel.

Note: The colors you mix will most likely not look exactly as on the graphic. The color wheel graphic shows the basic representation of the color, but in real life we have various different forms of each color and will get various different results as we mix them. It takes practice and experimentation to figure out how to get an exact form of a color such as the ones shown on the graphic.

Color Theory Terms

Hue: This is what we call the main aspect of the color. It's the, well, color of the color. It's red, blue, orange, purple etc. Hue describes the main characteristic of the color. In the art world, we use this word to describe the color regardless of its variation. And a hue can have many variations.

Warm and Cool Colors: On one side of the color wheel you will find the warm colors related to red and yellow and on the other side you will see the cool colors related to blue and green. The "temperature" of a color is a psychological reaction that we have when we look at the color. For instance, red or yellow generally reminds people of fire, and blue tends to make us think of water or glaciers. We pay attention to the temperature of colors as artists because it can have a big impact on the feeling or emotion of a piece when completed. A warm painting of an old lady with lots of oranges and yellows may remind you of your grandmother sitting by the fire telling you stories, while the same painting in blues and greens just might put a different light on her personality; if she doesn't look like she's suffering in wintertime she might make one feel that she is cold-hearted instead. I believe temperature is very important in the art of face-up and will be referring to it a lot throughout this book.

The color on the left is much warmer than the color on the right.

Note: If there is ever a question as to which is the warmer or cooler of two or more colors, a fun psychological exercise might help. Just ask yourself, "If these colors really have temperature, which one would I rather touch?"

Complementary Colors: The complementary of a color is located on the exact opposite side of the Color Wheel. Have you ever been told that your outfit "clashes?" This is what complementary colors do. Red could not be more different from green and the same goes for blue versus orange and purple versus yellow. When you put these colors side by side they go crazy. When they are especially intense they will play with your eyes and look as if they are moving. You might notice painters doing this when they want the painting to look loud and make you, the viewer, feel alert. If the colors are less intense, they can be placed together without looking too crazy and make an interesting effect for your eyes to savor. In the art of face-up you will be making the important decision whether to put complementary colors together or not. For instance, my doll Abbot's face-up is blushed with cool pinks (as seen in the photo on the next page). He is a very calm and cool character even before he received his face-up. So in order to add a little intrigue to the mix, I chose his bright green eyes, that are highly reflective, to contrast all that pink. If you ever need to know what the complementary of a certain color is, just look right across the Color Wheel.

Red and green are opposite on the color wheel and therefore are complimentary.

In this photo the bright green eyes complement the pink eye shadow and lips.

Analogous: This is the opposite idea of the complementary colors. Analogous colors sit side by side on the Color Wheel. Since they are so close in relation, they don't "fight" with each other like complementary colors do. Their effect is calming and can be used as the central idea in a face-up if you wish. For instance, a doll might have blue eye shadow with green eyes.

Analogous colors like blue and green sit next to each other on the color wheel.

Value: This is one of the most important aspects of art and should be taken just as seriously in face-up. Value is the lightness and darkness of a color. Think of a black and white photograph. The images in the photo are apparent because it is filled with various levels of value. My college art professor used to tell us that 99 percent of the time, value is the reason our eyes can decipher an object from its background. In color mixing, value can be increased by adding white and decreased by adding black. Paying attention to the distribution of value is very important in face-up because since the resin is such a smooth, even-toned, and somewhat translucent material it can be hard to decipher how it is shaped when viewed in strong light. As we blush the resin, we want to shade areas that need a little extra shadow like nostrils, eye sockets, etc. to make sure they appear at a glance and also to add the illusion of depth to the object that may not have been there prior. See pictures of Abbot's face in the photo be-low. Value is also extremely relevant to anything you might add to your doll, like tattoos. Two different colors side by side in the same value won't appear very distinguished unless the values are altered.

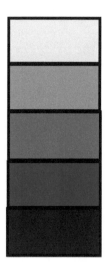

A Scale of grey Values

Above: Before and after Abbot's face-up. Darker values are used to blush the deep valleys of the sculpture to make them more apparent, particularly between the lips.

Intensity: is the brightness and dullness of a color. Also known as Saturation. How pink is that pink? Is it like hot pink or is it so dull it's almost brown? Intensity is closely related to temperature. The intensity of a color can be lowered by either adding grey or mixing it with its complementary color, the two colors will neutralize each other and become duller. The way to raise the intensity of a color is to place it next to a less intense color and let it show it's brilliance by comparison. With colors almost all things are relative.

> *The pink on the left is more intense than the pink on the right.*

Monochromatic: You might just choose to use one color in your face-up and nothing else! That would be a monochromatic face-up. In painting, the artist will choose one color with the addition of black and white to manipulate the color's value, and make a whole picture in that one hue. I think this can probably be achieved in face-up and the option is certainly there for you. It would be most authentic to use variations of the color of the resin to shade and highlight the face.

Optical Blending: happens when an artist places two colors side by side, like red and blue, and, when viewed from a distance, the eye perceives it automatically as a mixed color (purple). When you watch TV or look at a magazine, optical blending is doing its job. An image on television is made up of thousands of dots of light in only a few colors. When they come together and move around as they do, all your brain knows is that there is an image there. Print is very similar, except in this case it is thousands of dots of ink in only a few colors making the image. Your eyes are doing all the work. The famous painting *A Sunday Afternoon on the Island of La Grande Jatte* by Georges Seurat uses tiny dots of paint to make the image. Hmm, I wonder how we can use this in face-up.

Tonality: is the dominance of one color in an entire piece. It shows the importance of the color despite the presence of others. But all other colors should share this color in common. Imagine a doll face with purple eyes and a painted color scheme of reds and blues, and possibly a planned-out scheme of hair and clothes in these colors as well. An easy way to find out which colors to use is to refer to the color wheel, find your important color, and then select the colors to each side of it as the supporting colors.

Know Your Colors: What to Expect

As a devoted painter I can't help but use the "paint tube" color names. They are quite different from browsing the interior décor paint or the bottled craft paint section of the store. These are the terms that artists use, so I recommend getting to know them if you plan to hang out in our league for any amount of time. The graphic to the right may not match up exactly with the color in real life, but hopefully it will give you an idea as to what the colors are. These are the colors I use in almost all of my projects. The colors "light Pink" and "Light Blue" refer to pastel sticks that I recommend using. The rest are a recommended collection of both paint and pastel. Viridian is optional.

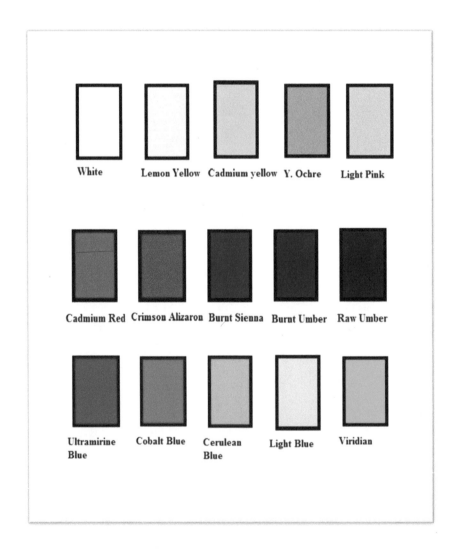

Chapter 5

Look at those Rosy Cheeks!

Using Pastels

The more pastel colors you have, the more freedom you will have to create different effects. You can start with the cheaper basic color sets but you may find yourself wanting more!

Avoid the type called "oil pastels," which are moist and look like crayons, they won't work.

Use the ones called soft pastels or nupastels. These look like richly colored chalk and are bone dry. The only difference is that nupastels are compatible with water and can be used as watercolor cakes. Hmm, I wonder how that would look on a doll face—feel free to give it a try!

I use nupastels every time. If kept dry they act exactly like regular soft pastels. This is where your craft knife comes in. Also grab either a sheet of paper or a dish you have dubbed as your pastel palette. Holding the pastel over the palette, gently scrape the knife along the edge of the pastel stick—as if you're trying to sharpen a piece of wood. But be gentle, and you only need a tiny pile of powder to do a face-up—thus the pastels will last you a VERY long time. You may never need to buy any more unless you choose to paint faces professionally and have a long waiting list of customers. You may want to do the shaving before putting your glove on, or else the pastel powder might rub off and dirty your glove while you're holding it. Keep the glove clean so you can use it to hold the doll head. Pick a nice variety of colors to start with. You can stick to primary colors and just mix secondary colors as needed. This is recommended, as your face-up will look softer, more natural, and more personalized if you mix your colors and not just use them in their purest forms (unless it is your professional choice as an artist to represent the colors in this way. You are certainly entitled to do as

you wish). You can read a bit about the art of color mixing in the next section. Of course, I definitely start with more color than just red, yellow, and blue. But colors like orange I can mix if I need it.

I always start with these basic colors and may add and subtract, depending on my plan for the design: Light Pink, Light Blue, Dark Blue, Cadmium Red, Cadmium Yellow, Yellow Ochre, Burnt Sienna, and Raw Sienna. Note: I have a large, expensive set of pastels with many color choices, but I pick and choose my colors carefully rather than spread all of them on the palette. Once you get to know the colors (and do feel free to test them on paper to see how they really look), you will decide which you find the most useful and will most likely use for each face-up project. Some brands might be courteous enough to provide a graph with names of the colors provided. But if not, never fear. I have provided a chart in Chapter 4 (page 35) to show you what to look for if you read words like "burnt sienna" and have no idea what I'm talking about. The most important thing is for you to know how you want your face-up to look and choose the color you think will best suit your idea.

Mixing Pastel Colors

This is similar to mixing paint except most of the time you won't need white. I never use white because I've only had pale dolls so far and only worked light to dark. Also, my white pastel sticks don't seem to shave a very fine powder. If your doll is dark, you may want to use white if you are highlighting cheekbones or something. If your white pastel stick shaves off tiny "pebbles" instead of powder then use a hammer or other hard smooth object that can gently grind the pebbles into a fine powder (but do this on a sheet of paper upon the table and NOT on your glass or porcelain palette).

The good news about mixing pastels is that it should be easier than paint and require less control. We are working light to dark and the gradual transformation should happen gracefully with little to no potential for mistake. You should not have to worry much about a color getting too dark as long as you keep the dark pastels aside until you are ready for them.

To get started, it shouldn't take more than your choice of red, pink, and/or yellow for a basic fleshy blush. Once again, if it's too reddish, you can add more yellow with a light blue. But this time you also have the option of using light green.

Remember red and green are complimentary and neutralize each other when mixed. One time when I had my doll's cheeks blushed reddish and sealed, I later experimentally brushed some light green onto the cheekbones and, instead of looking green, it lightened up the red area and acted more like a highlight. You can keep this method in mind if you sealed a reddish color in place and then later decide that you think it's too red. The green sort of acts like an eraser even though the red underneath is not going anywhere.

Mixing pastels is basically self-explanatory. If you want bright colors then mix bright colors, keeping the darker ones out. If you want a secondary color and have all three primary (red, yellow, and blue) then you can mix it. Refer back to the color wheel on the first page of Chapter 4 to find out how to mix all basic colors.

Light pink, cadmium red, and a little blue is being mixed here.

You can test the pastel color on paper to see how it looks. You can also brush a little on paper or a towel to lighten the amount of dust that will go onto the doll head.

To mix, use the brush to drag a little of each colored powder to a new pile somewhere on the palette and then gently stomp the edge of the brush bristles over the new pile to mix the colors together. I always use a small flat brush for my blushing, with bristles stiff enough to hold their ground while stomping the powder. To clean the brush, no need to get water involved. Just dust it across a dry paper towel to remove all the powder and then you can use the same brush for the next pastel color. Avoid getting any of your pastel brushes wet while they are in use. They may not spread pastel very well until they are dry again (and a wet brush will activate the "watercolor" function in nupastels). But feel free to wash them in water at the end of the day if you want to. I don't do that, but the option is there for you.

Note: You can assign one brush to each color category: reds, blues, blacks, etc. This may save you from having to worry about cleaning the brush before moving on to the next color. If not, it should not be too difficult to brush the color away on a towel.

Keep in mind: mixing regular primary blue, for instance, with primary red when looking for a purple, you will get a dark cool purple. This is also true for paint. If you are looking for a warm Easter-like lavender then look to colors like crimson alizarin (or some other red-violet) with a warm blue, like cobalt. This will give you a friendly lavender. You may have to experiment with different variations of the colors to get what you are looking for.

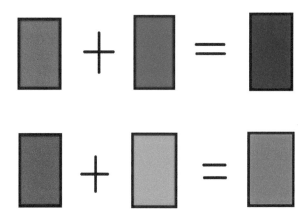

Above: Example of the different variations of the same color. Different purples can be found when different reds and blues are mixed.

Layer 1

A great way to get warmed up without making any dramatic changes to the face just yet is to start with pure light pink (or light blue if the doll is a zombie or sea creature). Just dab the brush in the pink powder and start blushing the doll head where it counts: cheeks, eyes, nose, lips, and ears. This color is so light, you may barely see it. This technique works as light-to-dark anyway, so don't try to force a dark color on it. Most colors don't want to be dark just yet. You have to layer them a few times to make them appear dark. I will explain about Layering in the next section. When using light pink, you shouldn't have to erase anything either. Light pink is a shy color and should not look at all loud or out of place in this stage no matter where it lands. But this first step will breathe a delicate feed of life into the "skin" of the doll and may also result in boosting your confidence. This color needs no control.

Try not to apply it very thickly or force the color to become darker, no matter how far into the layering process you get. The sealant's tooth can only hold so much powder. Each layer, separated by another coat of sealant, will add depth to the color. So go ahead and distribute the light pink to each facial landmark and let's seal it in place!

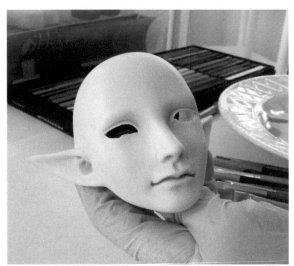

Layer 2

Now that you've sealed your first layer of pastel and let it dry, it should be permanent in a way that when you continue working, it should remain intact and untouched. If you erase anything of the next layer the light pink should still be there underneath. Now we're ready to increase the color depth. If pink is your thing and you're doing a soft "cutesy" look for your doll, you can feel free to do a second coat of pink or a mixture of a deeper pink using something like red-violet or crimson. I usually move on to using red at this point for a good basic look of realism. Unless your character is undead, you'll proba-

bly agree on fleshy reddish cheeks and lips. You can use pure red for a bright and intense look or tone it down by mixing it with a yellow and/or a little brown. One of my favorite reddish mixes consists of cadmium red, light pink, and cadmium yellow. The color is so fresh and vibrant, I would call it "tropical pink" if I were to name it. I encourage you to try any mixture you want—you never know what you'll discover. Don't be afraid to try different browns, yellows, or even a little blue or violet in your mix. Remember to dust a little across a sheet of paper to see how it might look first (or remember that it can erase very easily off of

After first blushing the head with light pink, I move on to mixing a fleshy red tone for layer 2.

the doll head or the doll's head cap).

　　So give it a try! Add your new color wherever needed. If this is your cheek color, you have the option to spread it to the eyes, nose, ears, and lips, or you can mix a slightly different color for those. The main landmark in question for sharing this color, I would say, is the lips. Is your doll wearing "lipstick?" If so, the color may be a different mixture. If not, then they may look more natural if they share the same color as the rest of the face. Either way, unless you want your doll's lips to look pale, then this is where you should concentrate the color. When it's on the cheeks or around the eyes, it should be soft, with barely any edges showing—the blush should fade into the natural resin color gracefully. But lips, having blood close to the surface, should be rich with color and concentrated into the compact space that is the lips.

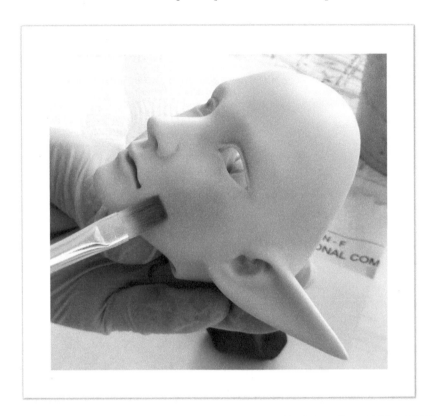

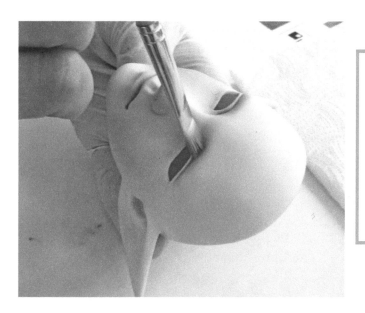

I start layer 2 by blushing my reds where I had previously blushed light pink. I always start with the cheeks, but you can use any order you want. As this layer spreads across the face you may find yourself excited to see that the doll is already beginning to look "alive!"

Use the Kneaded Eraser to Alter the Blushing

If you put some color on the cheeks and think, "Ug! That's way too bright!" Then this is where the kneaded eraser comes in. Squeeze a side of the kneaded eraser into a flat pad that you can use to dab at the color to take some of it away. You will probably notice that it makes the color spotty. This may or may not be a bad thing. If you don't want blotchy or spotty and prefer a perfectly soft color with edges that blend away gracefully, you can continue to erase most of it away, take the brush back up without dipping it back into the powder, and dust more on. This time there is less powder on the brush and you may attain a blush that is the right thickness. If the blotchy look was not so bad, you can continue to dab the eraser as needed and switch back to the brush to dust and repeat until the area has a perfect look.

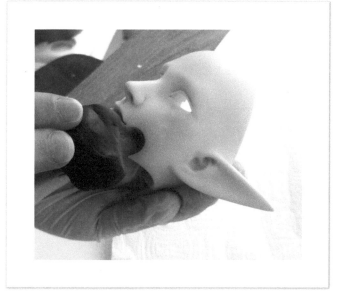

Do Your Rounds

Sealant, if you are using an imported brand, is expensive. As you get a handle on the process, you will find ways of getting the most out of every layer of sealant. I would not blush the cheeks—seal—blush the nose—seal—and then shade the eye sockets and seal again. That would not be very economical and it would make the face-up take much longer than needed. That's why I say, "Do your rounds." Give attention to each facial landmark before sealing each time. In one layer, move around the entire face, taking care not to let your elements step on each other's toes (if they are not supposed to).

Try not to over-blush areas too thickly in one layer or you will overload the "tooth" of the sealant layer and all the excess pastel will fall off or build up and look dirty on the surface of the resin. So lay down a decent amount of color on each landmark that needs it, stop, and then seal. Now some landmarks may be finished for now or they may be ready for the next wave of color. So do your rounds. Ears, eyes, lips, cheeks—keep laying color where it is still needed.

Let's say you have put down enough pastel everywhere and are done with them. Congrats! Now may be time to take up the watercolor pencils or acrylic paint. Go ahead and draw your eyelashes, eyebrow hair, lip lines, facial tattoo, etc., then seal again to protect your painstakingly-drawn lines! What's that? You think the eyes could use more eye shadow? That's fine—the art of face-up is totally flexible! Go back to working on the pastel again if needed. The very last step, which does NOT need to be sealed afterward, is the gloss you'll probably apply to the lips and eyes. If you seal again after doing that then your shiny surface will disappear, and I've proven that for myself. I had to put on another coat of gloss to get the shiny look back. That is the basic idea. You'll mix pastels and paint and apply them in layers, doing your rounds, until you are satisfied with your doll's appearance. You are the boss! But we're not done yet. Let's move on to the third layer.

Layer 3 and Beyond

Layer 1 was just simple light pink (or whatever alternative color you chose). In layer 2, we added some more intense reds or pinks mixed with yellows or browns and distributed these colors where necessary. I usually distribute my new reddish color to every facial landmark. What I am left with is quite a lively little fellow or lady. If you want to stop here, you may be able to do it if you think your character is lively enough. And from here we would draw eyebrows and lashes and any other embellishments needed to make the face complete. But I always go on to add shading and other color elements to my face-up before I'm finished with the pastels. This is where it may get complicated. Not scary-complicated, but I always lose track of how many times I've sealed. That's why I call it "Layer 3 and Beyond."

Enhancing the Face with Color Elements

Anything listed here is free to bend into your unique plan. There is no right or wrong way to order these steps. I will tell you what I do and usually about when I do them, but please remember that you have the freedom to skip or reorder anything beyond this point, unless a specific effect needs to happen in its own order—I'll let you know. The only step that should definitely be in its ordered place is the gloss at the very end of the process. Unless the gloss is applied last, any sealing you do afterward will make the gloss disappear and you'll have to reapply it. Here is a general list of techniques that I use to create illusions on a doll's face. Remember you can blush, seal, and repeat as needed on just about all effects to make them darker.

<u>Blue on the Nose Bridge:</u> Light blue is what I suggest for this element. Unless your

doll is a special resin color like chocolate or blue, then I recommend light blue. For darker skin tones, you may have to use your own discretion on color mixing for this effect. Just use your smallest blushing brush, get some light blue on it, and apply it delicately to the sides of the bridge of the nose right by the eyes. Look into the mirror to find what I'm referring to. Do you see a blue or violet vein right there on the nose bridge by your eye sockets? It may be harder to see in dark-skinned people. I'm assuming your doll is light-skinned, as are the majority of BJD's, but if not, and if you are confused by this, or just don't like the idea, then you can skip it as you please. It's not super important, but it is one effect I use every time. Just having that little flash of cold color there to contrast whatever warmer color I used for eye shadow makes an interesting shift to dazzle my own eyes whenever I look at my dolls' faces. And this effect doesn't ever seem erratic or out of place either. If anything, it may deepen the nose bridge as cool colors tend to recede and warm colors jump forward. You may have to use your kneaded eraser and re-blush as needed to make sure these two spots are symmetrically straight when looking at the face from the front. This may or may not be a problem for you—just keep trying if it is and you'll get it eventually.

Shade the Eye Sockets: Do you want your doll's eye sockets to be shaded? Do you want a warm shade or cool shade? I generally shade my eye sockets warmly. In this case I used cadmium red, burnt sienna, and yellow ochre. I use my new color to go over what I've already done in Layer 2, covering basically the entire eye socket—top and bottom lids and usually all the way up to where I plan to draw the eyebrows. If you want a cooler look, then I would suggest adding a blue, raw umber, and/or purple. I used these colors when it came time to focus a little on the lid creases. Make sure to

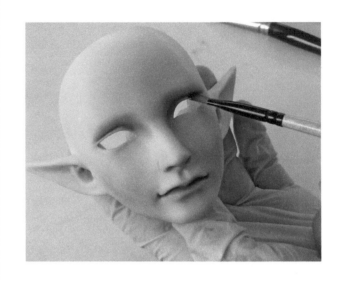

focus plenty of color into the lid creases if your doll has them. Remember not to overdo it. If you don't feel the color is dark enough, then you'll have to add more in the next layer of sealant.

Hue doesn't matter!

Well maybe it does a little, considering that you want your doll to wear certain colors. When I speak of warm and cool colors, remember that ALL colors have warm and cool variations. I'm not forcing you to use tones of "beige." You can use any color of the rainbow for eye shadow, blush, etc. For example, if you were to choose blue eye shadow then that is perfectly acceptable—but the question of temperature will still be there.

Shade the Deepest Landmarks: Your shading color can be warm or cool. In this case I used a little of both—cool and dark reds and browns with a little blue thrown in. Load up your brush and stick it right up the doll's nose! Actually the nose may vary. Some dolls have shallow nostrils and some have deep. If they are shallow, you may want to create the illusion of depth by using the shading color to blush the nostrils. If your doll has very deep nostrils and the depth is already apparent, then you can skip this part if you

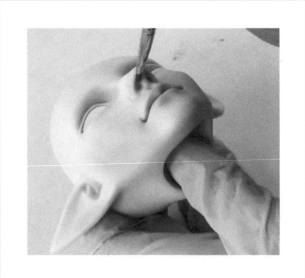

want. Other than that, I would shade the mouth between the lips, the deep parts of the ears, and possibly the eye creases and the sockets above the eyeball close to the nose if you want them to appear deeper. Note: Let's say you shaded the nostrils and wish you hadn't. Remember you have a very handy erasing tool in the kneaded eraser! You can shape it the way you need to stick it up the doll's nose and rub out most or all of the color.

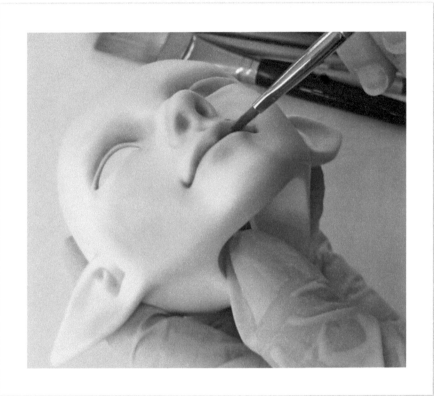

The deepest landmarks, like the nostrils, may need a little extra shading to make them apparent.

Lips: Are your doll's lips pale or flushed? Is he/she wearing lipstick? Are the edges of the lip color sharp or soft? As a basic rule, I start by shading the lip crease with a shadowy color. The shadow color may be warm or cool depending on what you are going for. Then I do a pinkish/reddish blush for my general color. The top lip color usually comes out softer than the bottom lip for me, but you can keep adding color to darken as you wish. Next I will usually focus a darker/redder color into the crease near the middle and let it come out onto the bottom lip, staying to the center, so the lip has a softer color on the sides and darker color to the center.

Shade the Lip crease: I believe in blushing a shady color into the lip crease rather than draw a stark line in dark paint (unless you want your doll to look more anime). This step may need to be applied to a layer separate from the pinkish lip color. Effects can be achieved by ordering this layer with the pinkish layer. It's up to you whether to layer the shade over or under the lip color.

Widen the Mouth Corners? This one may be needed if your doll's lip crease isn't shady enough. I don't like to draw a line across the mouth anymore because it usually looks too obvious. I shade with pastels if needed and then, if the mouth doesn't look as wide as I want, I will use paint to draw short tiny lines or dots on the corners, disappearing into the depth of the crease. Even if the crease is shallow, I would still only use tiny extensions on the corners. And I avoid using stark black. Before making the color decision, think about what dark brown, blue, or maroon can do for your lip crease. Dark blue could possibly make the crease look deeper because, remember, cool colors recede.

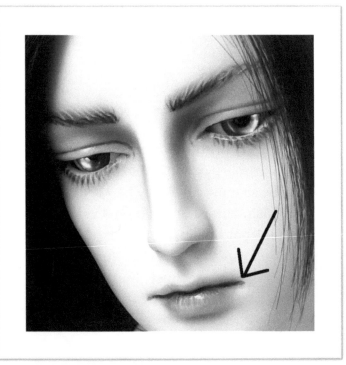

Blue on the Lips? I recently noticed on real people that a little blue might be visible on the sides of the bottom lip. I illustrated this technique on Laiska (seen in the picture at right). It's similar to the technique for putting light blue on the nose bridge. This can be applied early or late in the face up depending on what you are doing. It might be best to use it early if you have a complex lip design in mind.

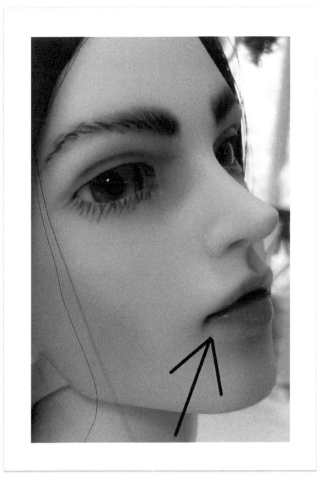

Eyebrows: If you are nervous about starting your eyebrows, you can start your design by using a very light pastel or thin line with a light watercolor pencil. Yellow or light blue are excellent choices. Keep in mind that your practice color may glow through or alter the true color you choose for your eyebrows. This may or may not work in your favor. For instance, if your doll is going to be red-haired, like Raivo, then yellow ochre should be a good choice of practice color (as seen in the photo below). If your doll is going to have black hair, then I would choose light blue. After applying your practice marks, you can either seal them in place to be colored over later or you can erase them, now knowing what you have in mind, and do the actual eyebrows. Either way, I suspect your eyebrows will be accomplished over the course of a few layers of color. There will be more information on eyebrows in Chapter 7.

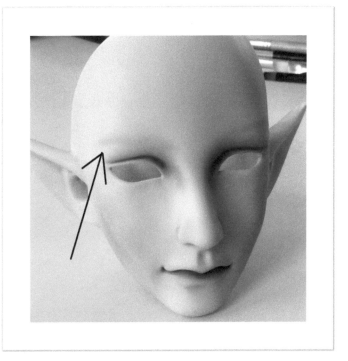

<u>Shade the Sides of the Nose:</u> This one is totally optional. It may apply only if your doll has a big broad nose. If your doll's style is closer to Anime and barely has one, or if it just has a little cutesy nose then you may want to skip this idea. My doll, Abbot, has a nice big nose, and because it is resin and not real flesh, I was concerned that his nose shape would not be apparent. The resin, unlike real flesh, is smooth and evenly toned all over which is why we are blushing it in the first place. I was sure that if I did not do something, his nose would be washed out in most lights. So I used a pinkish beige to shade the sides of his nose. It is a cool pink color to bring some life into that cold hard resin and also to make the sides of his nose recede so that the bridge could stand out proudly. As you can see in the lower photo I have done the same for Raivo.

Blushed Eyelashes: I like doing this because it can make my eyelashes look soft or smoky (depending on how dark I make it). This can also act as your actual eyelashes if you are choosing not to draw lines. You can make the color apparent or you can just use a little extra fleshy pink if you want. In the photos, I chose to blush Raivo's lower eyelid with a mixture of ultramarine blue and raw umber. Feel free to add and subtract color as you please. It's simple, hard to mess up, and easy to correct with

an eraser. Just carefully blush the edges of the lid with your chosen color. Do you want your color to be long or short? Do you want it to stretch back beyond the eyes like an ancient Egyptian? Do you want the color to reach all the way to the inside corner of the eye or stop midway? Do you want a warm or cool color? On Raivo's bottom lid I chose a cool blue to cooperate with his cool green eyes, and a warm beige color to contrast with them on the upper eyelid. Feel free to play around.

Hairline, Sideburns, Beard, Mustache, and Five 'o Clock Shadow: All of these can be accomplished the same as the Awesome Eyebrows technique covered in Chapter 7. I assume you want to match these things to the wig. If so, have your wig nearby and start

experimenting with color matching. Blush your hair color onto the face in the shape of the body of hair. If you need help with shapes then you can consult the internet for pictures of men with beards etc. You can also find out how hairlines are different on men and women and how they differ on various head shapes. The same goes for five 'o clock shadows; you'll have to decide how dark or light it is, usually a faint blushing of blue around the chin and jaw will usually do it. For beards and

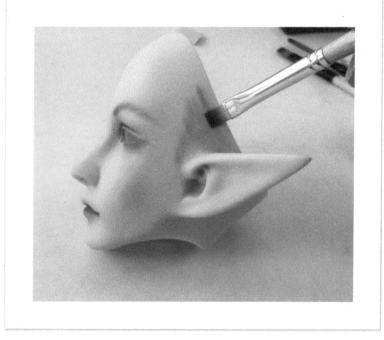

hairlines you will most likely have to layer them a few times to get the value that you need and then later add watercolor pencil and/or paint lines. Remember to pay attention to these hairlines as part of the pastel process as you do your rounds to save time and sealant.

For sideburns and hairlines, blush the pastel hair color in flowing drifts in the direction the hair grows (or hangs depending on the style). Next you can create the illusion of hair by erasing lines into the pastel in the same rhythm. Later, watercolor pencils and/or paint lines can be added.

Tattoo: Since this one is most likely going to be high detail and nerve-wracking (depending on your skill and confidence level), I give you permission to focus on this task and not worry about doing your other rounds while you work. In fact, I would personally draw the tattoo last, right before glossing. If this is an ice cream sundae then the tattoo should be the whipped cream and the gloss should be the cherry. It's best to practice your design on paper for as long as you need before trying it on the doll. I can't give you much advice, besides practice and do a light pre-drawing before using the dark colors, because the tattoo is limited by your imagination. I assume it will either be a line drawing or colored in with pastel or paint. If it is colored in, then I would add the colors FIRST and then layer the black outlines on top. Take your time and good luck!

I think that about covers it for Color Elements. The next step would be the line work. So grab your paints and watercolor pencils and let's get to it!

Chapter 6

Line Work

We've pretty much completed our pastels and it was a breeze, right? You may be finished with them completely by now, but keep them near just in case you forgot something. You can always continue with them later, even after starting line work.

Line Quality

If you have or are taking a good college art class, you may find yourself somewhere between slightly annoyed and a breaking point over an aspect a good art teacher will insist upon. But try not to snap because the teacher knows what she/he is talking about and that's usually Line Quality. Consider it one of the most important aspects of art. We, who are looking at art, want to see beautiful lines, not ugly ones. How many times have you looked at someone's handwriting and made a mental note, regardless of intensity, on how beautiful or hideous it is? The line must be graceful and purposeful, like it knows where it's going and what it wants to do. It must have thick points and thin points and dance on the page like a ribbon on the wind. Bad line quality is usually the line that is hesitant and awkward. This aspect of art can be hard to master and even harder to explain in all of its relevancies. So I'm just going to go straight into how we can apply this to the art of face-up.

Bad line quality done in the early stages of my face up practice.

Acrylic Paint

Tapered lines are good. The brush must come down firmly at the start of the line and then lift up as the line comes to an end. For eyelashes you'll want your lines to be uniform, each a copy of the last but they must vary in length depending on where they grow along the eye. The keys to getting good line quality is swiftness and moving your hand in to-the-point motions, knowing exactly where you want to go and following through. Don't be hesitant or lost, unsure of what you want the line to do or your lines may look like the eyelashes in the photo on the previous page at best. Ideally we are supposed to paint/draw with our arms, not our wrists or fingers. This idea is tricky in face-up, because it is such a tiny object and we usually don't want the eyelashes to stretch all the way to the doll's jaw. But try not to keep your arm, wrist, or hand too stationary. Your fingers alone can't do the work. In this case you want to control the line without being a control-freak. Don't come to a complete stop before lifting the brush or pencil and moving to the next line—remove the tool while in motion to get tapered ends. Breathe deeply and let the breath out as you follow through with the line. But don't hyperventilate by doing this on every line. You can take your time on each line, breathing deeply and slowly, or you can strike them all down rapidly using practiced uniform motions and your lines will show what you have done.

Consider your lines to be a recording of your motion. It will forever stand to tell future generations what you have done, how you are feeling, and how confident you are. Art can be a very romantic endeavor.

Color Mixing with Paint

Supplies needed: Paint Palette, Brushes (small sizes like 10/0 or 20/0), Paper towel, cup of water, acrylic paint thinner (prepared and mixed in a narrow-nozzle squirt bottle), mixing knife, cotton swabs, and a good collection of paint colors like these: Titanium White, Cadmium Yellow, Cadmium Red, Crimson Alizarin, Ultramarine Blue, and Raw Umber.

The first thing you should know is that acrylic dries fast. So don't leave paint on your brush and then take a break or it will dry into the bristles and your brush will be useless. This is why you have a cup of water. Just swish the brush around in the water, taking care not to rub the bristles against the bottom too hard, then wipe the brush on the paper towel to soak up the excess water. If you see color on the towel you should wash the brush again. Afterward, lay the brush neatly on the table to rest until it is needed again. Do NOT leave the brush standing bristle-down in the cup or the bristles will be ruined. If you take good care of your brushes, they will last much longer.

When you are ready to mix colors, put a small squirt of each color you will need on the palette. I put mine close to the edge and use the center as my playground for mixing. Go ahead and include every possible color you think you will need, even if you wind up not using it. It's always such an annoyance to have to pause to do more setting up right when we're "in the zone."

Let "Factory Black" Sleep at the Store

It's useful for certain impersonal chores but not for artistic expression. Any sort of "black" that is found at the store, no matter what fancy title it has, should probably be left alone. Of course, as an artist, you retain the right to do as you please, but in my professional opinion, and that of my college art professors, mixing your own black may prove to be more beautiful and rewarding. First, it will save you a few bucks not to buy it when you are already buying colors perfectly capable of mixing a better black. Secondly, black is a "dead" color. It has no personality. It's boring. It does not express the presence of other colors. Our black should be playful, radiant, and should interact with the others when placed next door. Don't believe me? Check out the examples below. The painting without the use of factory black is actually darker than the one that was! It wasn't until I got to college that I learned the value of mixing my own blacks. I will never go back, and I should know because darkness is my favorite subject.

The painting on the left was completed in 2008 and black was used in its creation. The painting on the right was completed in 2010 and no black was used whatsoever.

Release by Jesslyn Carver. 2008. Duplicated in 2010. Oil on Canvas.

The darkest color I can come up with is the simple combination of ultramarine blue and raw umber. This is a cool black. Interested in a warm black? Trade raw umber for burnt umber. Or you can trade the blue for crimson alizarin. Please take the liberty to experiment with your color mixing, you might discover on your own some great combinations! Some of them may not exactly be considered "black" but when it's the darkest color on your work of art, it shouldn't matter. If your doll is a Goth with heavy eye shadow, you need to use a dark value and this doesn't necessarily need to have anything to do with factory black.

Two different ways to mix black.

Use your mixing knife to scoop up part of the paint colors and relocate them to a new pile at the center of the palette. There is no formula for a "perfect" color, this is a right-brained industry and we go by feel until it comes out right. If there's not enough blue, add some, and vice versa for brown. Now neatly stir the knife around in the paint, grazing over it with the side of the blade, scooping it up again, and smearing it down until the colors are evenly mixed. If you are using a smooth palette with a thin metal mixing knife you should be able to lift the whole pile off the palette and turn it over a few times. You should also be able to scrape the pile together so that it doesn't spread too wide. Before you use the new color on the doll, you should put some thinner on it. I only thin half of the paint pile and save the un-thinned half for future color mixing. Use your squirt bottle to put one or two drops into the paint at a time.

Note: after drying, gouache paint reactivates when it is rewetted with water. This can ruin the paint job if it's not protected under sealant, but is convenient for saving the paint on your palette for later.

Now you can use your knife to mix the thinner into the paint. At first, put minimal thinner into the paint because you can always add another drop if you need it to be a little looser. There is no perfect formula for thinning. You should experiment with consistencies and see which looks best. It is a good idea to practice on paper or the doll's head cap. If the paint is too thin it will run and if it's too thick it will not make a thin or long enough line. Once you get the hang of dealing with paint, you will

later know how to judge when the paint is thinned enough—and even when you are a pro, it's always a good idea to do a few strokes on paper to make sure your lines are looking good. I recommend going ahead and mixing a black even if you don't want to use it in its pure form. You can mix it with other colors later to lower the value if you need to. Other than that, make sure you have white. White can be mixed with any color to raise the value and soften the intensity.

Mixing Flesh Tones

To mix a basic fleshy pink, the idea is to use white, cadmium red, and cadmium or lemon yellow. And then it's subject to alteration. For instance you can always add a little blue, brown, yellow ochre, and/or crimson alizarin. The best you can do is practice with colors like these to see what you can come up with. If you have trouble finding a certain tone then look closely at the color. I always ask myself, "What's missing?" Is the color too reddish? Maybe you should add more yellow to even it out. Does it look orange now? Keeping in mind that orange and blue are compliments, a tiny dot of blue can usually go a long way in neutralizing a potential flesh tone to a nice soft appearance. And remember to add white if you think the color is too dark. If the color is too yellow then you can do the opposite and add more red and or blue and white. If your doll's resin is a chocolate color and you're looking to make similar shades in paint, then you're going to be using more of your browns, blues, and reds, including crimson alizarin. Just mix more browns and possibly blues in than the white and yellows. Practice as much as you need—don't worry about wasting money/materials because you are learning and this part is very important.

The above color combination is the basic idea for mixing a peachy flesh tone.

Adding small dots of color at a time can slowly shift your color into different characteristics.

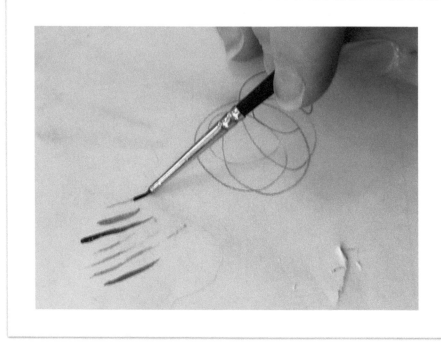

Making Marks

Practice making marks on paper for as long as you need. Mix up your color, add a little thinner to loosen it up, and then see what your paint and brush can do together. Find out how much paint on the brush is too much or too little. Know what is going to happen before it happens on the doll's face. Hold the doll head however is most comfortable for you. When doing the opposite side of the face from your favored hand, you may find it helpful to turn the head upside down. For instance, I'm right-handed and turn the head upside down to paint on the doll's right side. This side usually comes out better for me than right-handedly painting the doll's left side (which is closest to my right when right-side-up).

A good place to start would be the upper lid. Most people don't paint tally marks up there—it's not very realistic and may give your doll the classic porcelain doll look. Instead, we usually just paint the upper rim of the eye hole in a dark color. This will shade the eye nicely and won't reflect light back at the viewer, looking unfinished or hollow. When looking at the doll at an angle and from a distance, we can usually see this black paint as it creates the illusion that the doll does have upper eyelashes. Some people continue this painted eyelash color to the outside of the eyelid so it can be seen head-on.

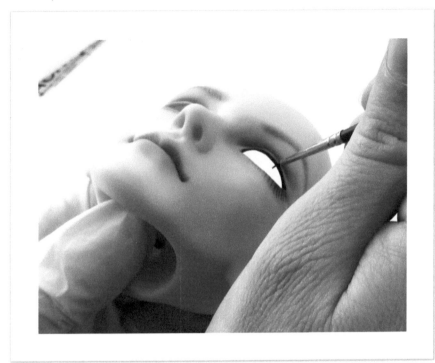

If painted thickly on the outside, the doll will look as if she has thick heavy eyelashes. Other than that, a lot of people later glue 3D eyelashes to the upper lid.

Next we can do the eyelash strokes on the bottom lid. You'll want to make each mark quickly even if you are going slow and taking it one line at a time. So go ahead and make the first eyelash or brow mark. Remember if you make a mistake, you can always erase paint with a drop of thinner on one end of a cotton swab, leaving the other end for drying. Act quickly if you make a mistake, because it is easier to erase while the paint is wet. But it's still not the end of the world if it dries. A dry line can still be erased if it has not been sealed.

Watercolor Pencils

This method may be easier or harder; everyone is different. It's a good idea to buy a set with as many colors as you can afford. You may find them sold individually; I buy these to stock up on the colors that did not come in my set or replace the colors I used up. If you want to buy all of your colors this way then please remember to get dark colors, possibly excluding black, and as many shades of light fleshy colors as possible, and don't forget white.

I find it harder to get good line quality out of pencils because of their lack of flexible bristles sliding across the object. When I first tried it I found that they made a bunch of grainy pencil lines and I went back to the brush. I didn't want a bunch of obvious pencil lines showing, I wanted to make illusions happen on my doll's face. But I eventually overcame my problem with the pencils and found that I just needed to be faster and lighter. So I hold the pencil in a loose way and quickly strike it along the bottom eyelid without thinking about anything. Once again I suggest you practice on paper first.

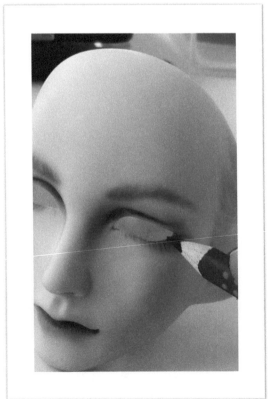

As far as color goes, this is all up to you. I would not use plain black. Instead I would use either a dark blue or maroon or something else. Some people like to use two or more colors for the eyelashes, like white to act as highlighted hairs and then dark, possibly with something in between. For Raivo's face-up, I used a light peachy pink to make empty "erased" lines through the pastel and then used dark maroon to contrast with the cool bluish pastel haze that I created earlier.

Keep in mind that these pencil lines are designed to run on contact with water. The color can be spread from the line and it will also intensify the color. Feel free to practice with this effect—you might discover an awesome new face-up technique. And also remember that this may work against you. If you plan to use paint in close proximity to your pencil lines, it would be a good idea to seal your pencil lines with sealant before putting any paint down or use and let the paint dry first before moving to watercolor pencils.

> Tip: After sharpening the colored pencil, the lead can be sharpened further by grazing the craft knife along the lead. Next it may be a good idea to rub the side of the lead against paper to remove dust or jagged pieces ready to fall off. Before I get started, I do a few warm-up strokes on the paper to make sure the tip of the lead is ready to go.

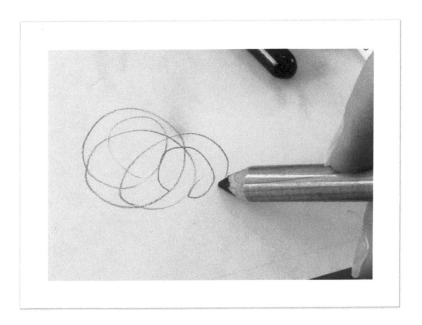

Practice Makes Perfect

Yes, that's right! You've heard it many times in your childhood, and I can't stress it to you enough now. If this is your first time in any sort of artsy endeavor, you will probably run into frustration. But don't lose heart and remember that even the professionals have frustration! I'm pretty sure most all face-up artists don't often keep their first try. I didn't. So just keep at it. Eventually you will paint a decent face-up!

Eyelash Tips

Don't be afraid to be playful with color, you never know what cool sort of illusion you might discover. I chose dark maroon pencil to draw Raivo's main eyelashes, because I knew he would be wearing green eyes. Because red and green are complementary colors, they tend to fight each other when in close range and will dazzle the eye in the process. For a calm and cool appearance you can use similar colors around the eye that are on the same side of the color wheel, like blue and green. This might make your character look a little calmer.

I used both pencil and paint in Raivo's eyelashes and brows. I added paint later to make his eyelashes a bit fuller. Notice that my paint lines are shorter. Pencil has the ability to go as far as you want and make for longer eyelashes. A paintbrush only has so much ammo before it runs out. So the choice is yours: are your eyelashes long and thin or short and thick? This is a matter of style with no right or wrong answer.

Eyelashes drawn with pencil.

Eyelashes drawn with paint.

If you've already drawn or painted your eyelashes or eyebrows, it's never too late to do another light dusting of pastel around the eyes. Of course you should first let your paint dry and seal again before doing this. The effect may soften your lines if you think they need it.

Whether you are using paint or pencil, you can erase using the acrylic thinner on a cotton swab. Put a drop or two of thinner on one end and leave the other end dry, which you can use to dry the area you erased. Other than that, you can also use the erasers to remove the pencil lines.

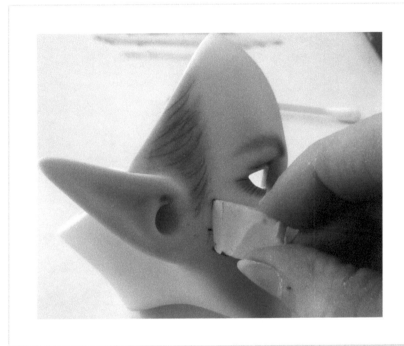

Watercolor pencil erases well with an eraser or acrylic paint thinner on a cotton swab.

Alternate Paint Option

You may be able to save money on paint if you'd like to try using your watercolor pencils as paint. You'll still need brushes and a cup of water for this. And your paint will work much better if you include the acrylic thinner! Just grab a sheet of paper, take your chosen watercolor pencil and lay the lead horizontally along the page. Now gently scribble the lead on the paper to make a nice dense block of color. This is your new water color cake! You can wet the cake down with water to activate the paint, but a drop of acrylic thinner works much better and lasts longer. Be conservative with the amount of water or thinner used to make your scribble last longer. Your pencil scribble is now paint! Go ahead and do some practice marks to see how it looks. Try every color of pencil you have to see how it turns out. And remember that you can still mix new colors by scribbling various pencils together before wetting.

One pro to this method is that it will be easy to control the amount of moisture on the brush. Another pro is the convenience of only having to buy and stock up on this medium, bypassing the paint. One con may be that the brush might dry fast and you'll frequently have to dip it back into the water and color (but acrylic thinner helps this a lot). Another con is that color mixing possibilities may be a little more limited and/or you may find yourself buying many more pencil colors to get the freedom you want (though a single pencil costs less than a tube of paint). But only you can decide if this method is right for you and I encourage you to weigh the pros and cons after conducting your own experiments.

Chapter 7

The Awesome Eyebrows Technique

When you are ready to tackle those eyebrows, you can start by making the shapes with a light color first before committing to your darker hair color. Now is the time to decide where your eyebrows are located and what sort of expression they are making. So locate the brow bone—the ridge that marks the top of the doll's skeletal eye socket (this may be less apparent in more cartoon-like dolls, so just do your best). For most people, the eyebrows grow here. Generally they start right where the eyes begin or are aligned with the sides of the nose and end a little after the eyes do. This is a common standard of beauty, but remember that you have full creative control over your unique character.

Is your character daring or sensitive? A basic idea for an emotional character might be to keep the eyebrows at an even level, perhaps turning upward at the inside corners. An angry character might keep his eyebrows low and drawn inward. A daring character's eyebrows might either be low or even on the inside corners with pointy peaks on the outsides. A soft-hearted or kind character's eyebrows might be hovering weightlessly with a little gentle upward arch. See the drawings to the right for inspiration.

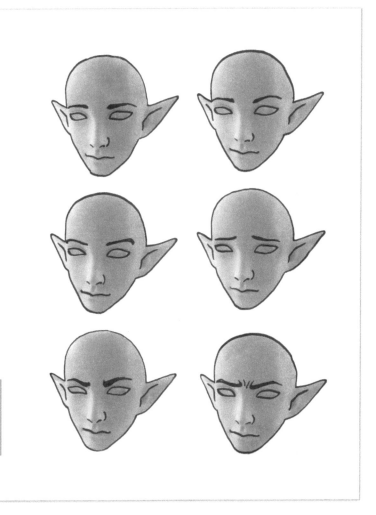

See how tense eyebrows draw together and relaxed eyebrows float apart.

Whether your doll's eyebrows are black, brown, or blonde, you'll notice that the first layer of color you put down will be very light. So you must work several layers of eyebrow color into your work plan. It is also acceptable to focus completely on the eyebrows after you're done with the rest of the face blushing, but this will result in more time and sealant used.

When you are ready, prepare your hair color for the eyebrows. Feel free to have his/her wig nearby for reference. Blush your color on in the shape and size that you want the eyebrows to be, using your eraser to refine the shape and size. Now put the head down for a moment.

Get your white plastic eraser and your craft knife. Put the eraser on the table and slice a slim wedge off of it as if you were slicing cheese. Now place the wedge on the table, lying flat, and, holding your knife at an angle, slice off the end of the wedge so that it has a beveled edge. Now you have a nifty new drawing tool!

Slice a beveled wedge off your white plastic eraser.

Use the sharp edge of your eraser wedge to draw swift lines in the pastel eyebrow shape, in the angle that hairs would grow. You can approach from the bottom, top, or both. If you prefer to approach from the top, this may resemble highlighted eyebrow hairs. Don't worry about making this perfect as it may not be obvious in the finished eyebrow and we will be repeating this step several times between sealant sprays until the eyebrows are dark enough. But if you do happen to make a mistake-- fear not! Just brush on a little more pastel powder in the problem area to refill your erased lines again. Simple as that! I usually add paint and/or watercolor pencil lines to these eyebrows later, but this would be a wonderful method to create the illusion of hair lines if you are choosing not to use those other mediums in your face-up.

When you are happy with your lines you erased through the pastel, go ahead and seal. Once the face is dry again, repeat those last steps, blushing on more hair color to the eyebrows and "cutting" erased lines through the pastel. It may be a good idea to place your lines in different positions from the lines below, this will create a symphony of different levels flowing gracefully along the eyebrow. In order to achieve the value and shape that you want, this may take several layers. Just do as many as you need. Raivo's eyebrows took at least three layers of pastel to achieve.

Remember, if you need inspiration, you can always look closely at the faces of your friends and family or do an internet search for pictures of people to see how their eyebrows look and how they grow. You're an artist now and may find yourself collecting torrents of reference material!

How do they look? By now you can either call it a day on the eyebrows, or you can consult the next section on adding paint and pencil!

Using Paint and Pencil on the Eyebrows

When it comes to paint and pencil, you can use one or the other or both. I decided to use both on Raivo. The order in which you use them probably does not matter, they work both ways. In this case, I used pencils first, so that is what I'm going to talk about.

Watercolor Pencil for the Eyebrows

The first color I suggest should correspond with the resin color. This doesn't have to be difficult as I recommend buying as many different fleshy colors as you can because they are all helpful in the art of face-up. Whichever color you choose doesn't have to be perfect. Draw swift lines in the way that eyebrow hairs grow along the eyebrow shape. This acts in a similar way to the erasing trick except the lines are much finer. For Raivo, my color matches so well that when the line goes beyond the eyebrow, it vanishes and is unseen on the resin; therefore, I don't have to worry about perfection. Make the lines go all the way across the eyebrow. I like how it chops up the outside ends and really makes it look like

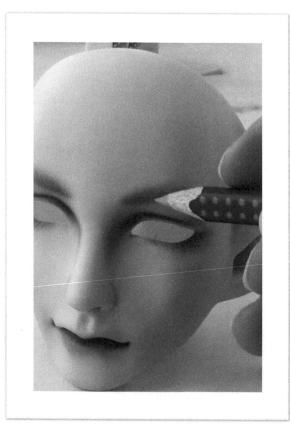

the hair is vanishing.

Next, choose a color close to your hair color and a few shades darker, or if you are feeling adventurous, you can use an odd color to accent the hair color like blue or maroon if your hair color is black. For Raivo's reddish eyebrows, I used a plain old dark brown that came in my set. Instead of going all the way across, I only made a few swift marks on the inside of the eyebrow and stopped before the center.

Remember when I was talking about studying faces and collecting reference material? I happen to remember a note I took when I was watching a movie about Elizabeth I Queen of England. I'm not sure if the actress was a natural red-head, but she sure looked authentic to me. I remember her reddish eyebrows glowing yellow in the soft indirect light. So I mimicked that effect using a yellow ochre watercolor pencil on the outside corners of Raivo's eyebrows. Just a few elegant strokes and it was done. So Raivo's eyebrows are constructed of a bottom layer of pastel, cut with an eraser, peachy pencil strokes throughout, dark brown pencil on the inside, raw pastel in the center, and then yellow ochre pencil on the outside corners. If you want to create a similar design you will have to make adjustments based on your chosen hair color. Just remember to choose a darker color related to the base color for the inside corner. It can be a darker value of the same color or it can be a tertiary color (found on the same side of the color wheel). And the outside highlighted color could be a higher value version or a higher value tertiary color.

Raivo's eyebrow colors are related in the sense that his base color contains much yellow and then I used pure yellow ochre to highlight the ends. Technically the highlight yellow is the same value as the base color and what is different is that the color now shifts into yellow as if light is reflecting differently here. I have included a drawing below to show the plan more clearly.

> *This is the basic idea of the construction and rhythm of the eyebrows. Use your own judgment when it comes to the direction of the pencil/brush strokes as all eyebrows grow differently.*

"Awesome Eyebrows" Layout Plan

Basic Pastel

Cut with Eraser

Pale colorpencil Lines

Dark colorpencil Lines

Light Hair color Lines

Acrylic Paint for the Eyebrows

For Raivo's face-up, this time I used minimal paint just to accentuate the darker hairs at the insides of his eyebrows. Acrylic always darkens as it dries, so it is good for darkening something like this if you feel the pastel and pencils are not enough. All I did was paint a few strokes on the inside corners, keeping my strokes near the bottom as if they were shadier, and stopped before reaching the center. And then I was done. Raivo's eyebrows are soft, detailed, and I did not feel overwhelmed with the task of painting fifty-something strokes, worrying about them all looking good, throughout both eyebrows.

Beards, Mustaches, and Hairlines

Use the same technique for beards and hairlines as the eyebrows. Blush the hair color in pastel wherever needed and in the shape needed. Feel free to consult the internet for different beard shape ideas etc. Use your eraser to cut lines into the pastel and then seal. Then repeat as needed until you are happy with the color/value. When you are done with pastels, you can use watercolor pencils or paint to draw intricate hair lines. Please note, in art, we don't usually draw every little hair in existence on the face or head. Just a few is usually enough to set the idea and then the human brain tends to fill in the rest.

On Raivo, I only made a few simple hairlines in pencil. Right in front of the ear, I like to add lovely waving hair lines for style. Don't bother making these perfectly symmetrical—no one's hair is symmetrical! But do practice your line quality on paper until you are confident and remember that the watercolor pencil erases easily. Abbot, my only doll who is not an elf, sports some rockin' sideburns. These are supposed to appear cropped, as if he trims them regularly, but I made a hair or two a little bit wavier and longer than the rest for a bit of style and imperfection. If your character is showing a little age, you can use white or gray lines in your eyebrows and facial hair.

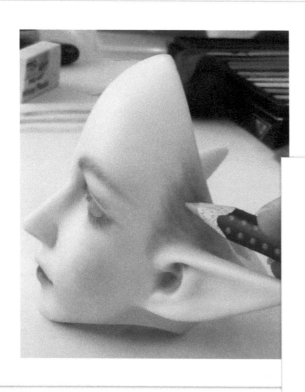

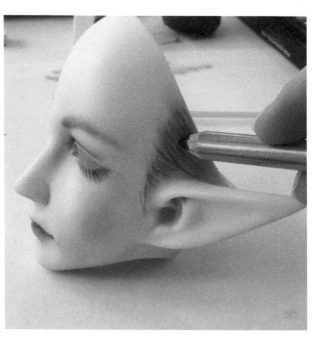

Just like the eyebrows, draw pale lines and dark lines through the hairline to create waves of various detail.

Abbot has variously sized hairs drawn into his sideburns for style and a feel of imper-fection.

Chapter 8

Finishing Up

Lip Lines

Lips lines are similar to the hair lines. I would pick a pencil or paint color that is similar to your base lip color, except a little darker and maybe more intense. A dainty set of pink lips would probably have deep rosy lines. Once again this can be done using either paint, pencil, or both. I've fallen in love with pencils for this job, though sometimes still add tiny lines in a more intensely-colored paint to the center of the bottom lip, mostly in the crease, peeking out to show the deepness of the doll's lips. You can also add pale watercolor pencil lines for highlights. These lines don't have to be perfectly symmetrical but I would take more care in evening them out than I did when working on the eyebrows. Start your pencil or paintbrush in the crease and drag it out away from the center as shown in the drawing below.

Draw Lip lines outward and away from the center of inside the crease.

Optional Effects

This is the time I would think about optional effects. I don't have very many optional mediums right now so if you have more than me you'll have to use your own judgment as to when they go into play. If you are using Pearlex Pigments glitter, now would be the time to use it. Also remember that this can be mixed into your pastel powder during your blushing process. You can blush it on wherever you want and then seal. Another idea is to use your gloss as a glue and glitter technique. Brush the gloss anywhere you want the glitter to appear and then sprinkle the glitter on as evenly as you can. This method is subject to invention. You can sprinkle it with your fingers, blow the glitter off your paintbrush and onto the gloss, or you can rig up a pouch from a loosely-woven piece of fabric and then shake it over the glossed area. You can gently blow away the excess glitter. You can give your doll glittery lips or eyes this way! You can also draw stylish swirls on the doll's face with the gloss and then sprinkle on the glitter.

This is also the time to draw your tattoos. If you are feeling tired after having completed the main face-up then feel free to put the tattoo project on hold for another day so you can tackle it later when you are rested up! Remember to take your time, practice, and good luck!

The Final Seal

When you have everything looking great and are finished with all that pastel and painting then you need to seal one more time to make sure your work is protected. So go ahead!

The Finishing Touch: Moisture

Now get out your gloss and whatever paint brush you think will be best. I always use a round line-drawing brush which is a little larger than the one I used to paint lines. The gloss is easy, just dip the brush directly into the bottle and brush it onto the lips, eyes, and anywhere else you see fit. Don't make it too thick. It won't be very shiny on this round if you are using the same kind as me (Liquitex Gloss Varnish). It takes at least thirty minutes for a coat to dry and then I add another coat and possibly a third if I want shinier lips. Once you are satisfied, let the final coat dry and then your doll head is ready to be reattached! Whew!

*"Feels good to get a fresh face-up
and a haircut, doesn't it?"*

Protecting the Face-UP

After all that work, you're going to want this face-up to last for a long time.

<u>The #1 rule</u> is not to touch the face! This is the easiest way to keep it clean. Whether you realize it or not there are oils on your fingertips that will show up on resin as dark smudges even better than other surfaces you touched. The best way to clean these fingerprints off is to buff it off with a Magic Eraser sponge. I hear some doll collectors are so careful with their precious resin people that they only handle the dolls when wearing gloves. You can go that far if you want, but I like to carry my dolls around and move them and hold them and enjoy them. I don't bother wearing gloves, of course. And my routine is ok because I don't touch the face. Ever. When I reposition the head I will either grab the top of their head which is covered by a wig or gently place my thumb under their chin and forefinger atop the wig. And I do wash my hands before touching them. When repositioning their body, I take advantage of the fact that they are usually wearing long-sleeved shirts or pants. But some aren't and I don't worry about it—every once in a while when I see a smudge on my doll's arm or leg I will just clean it off and move on. When I notice my doll's face collecting dust I use a single soft clean feather to dust it off. This also works well for dusting off the eyeballs. I keep a designated face-dusting-feather around for the job.

#2: You can further protect the face-up by not packing them into their box where something will be rubbing against their face. It might be a good idea to buy a protective face mask which can be found on the internet. Or perhaps you can rig up some sort of bubbly helmet to place over their face when they are packed up.

#3: Keep them out of direct sunlight. I don't think this protects the face up, but it does prolong the newness of the resin. If the doll is in the sun a lot, its resin will eventually turn yellow. It turns yellow naturally as it ages anyway, so don't let that bother you. It should not alter the beauty or value of the doll much if at all. The best way to deal with the resin's aged color is to accommodate it by updating the face up and/or outfit. Let your doll wear his/her new color proudly!

Inserting the eyes

I'm including this section based on an event in which some of my face up commission customers asked me to apply the eyes to their doll head for them. I want to encourage you to learn to do this yourself as it is not only necessary but fun to pose the eyes in different ways to change your doll's expression.

Eye Putty: There are a few options, but very few that I would choose! There is a kind that is white, I don't know what it's called or if there are various different forms of white eye putty, but I would stay away from this as I have seen it harden within the doll head and require sanding to remove it.

Some people have found that silicone waterproof earplugs make for good eye putty, and it does, but I don't like the greasy residue feeling it leaves behind on my hands and the doll head. Also I have been told that silicone earplugs will ruin silicone eyes, so please be careful if you want to use these things together.

My favorite eye putty of all is the green-colored sticky tack made by Faber-Castell. It seems to last a long time, is very sticky, and does not leave residue behind. Sometimes it will leave a little bit stuck to the resin but is easily removed by dabbing the traces away with a larger lump of it. I have trouble finding it in stores, so I get mine from online BJD supply stores. This is the type of putty shown in the photos.

First break off two pieces of putty and roll them into little snakes. There is no perfect amount, just use your best judgement based on the size of the eyes, you can add more if need be.

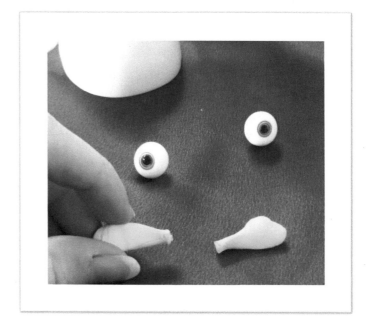

Now wrap it around the eye so that it looks like a doughnut. Keep it on the sides but pushed backward a little.

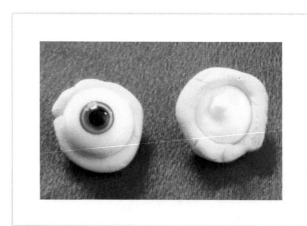

Insert the eye into the eye socket. Position the eye in the pose you want. Make sure there is no putty showing at the front of the eye. If the putty is too far forward, it may hold the eye back from the opening, resulting in the dolls eyes looking, shadowed, empty, and just plain unnatural.

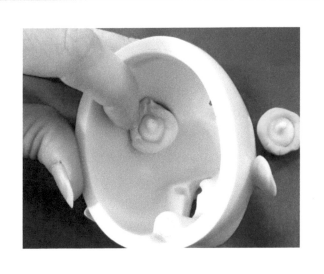

Use your fingers to push the putty onto the resin so that it traps the eyeball between itself and the doll head.

As you work the putty into position, remember to keep a watch on the front of the eyeball to make sure that it remains in the position you want. Do the same for the second eye. Once they are in, you may still be able to budge the eyes to perfect the doll's gaze, but this may loosen the putty, so be careful.

Below are some examples to show your freedom of expression through the doll's eyes. Just to further stress this freedom to you, I will tell you that I have a small childish doll named Kalle, who has her eyes positioned slightly crossed! It was a conscious idea I used to develop her physical character. Her right eye is only slightly leaning more inward than I would normally do. This is who Kalle is. She will always look like this.

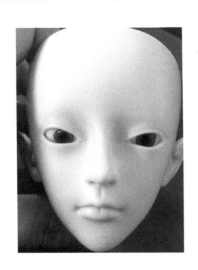
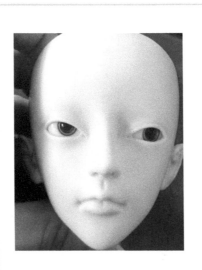

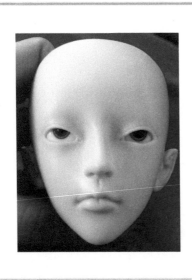
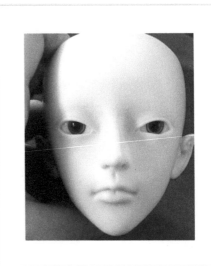

About the Author

I was born with the natural personality of an artist. That's not saying I was born making masterpieces like a child prodigy—no—but I've always had a strange and eccentric little personality and a lot of ideas and fantasy in my head. I earned my skills the hard way like normal kids, but it was always pretty clear that I would grow up to choose an art career. So I practiced a LOT from the age of--let's say--10 and my ambition rose from there. I jumped into oil painting after spending a little time with a neighbor who introduced me to acrylic first. But oil soon became my life's love and still is. I was able to refine my skill when I attended college in my twenties. My favorite artists are Jan Vermeer and similar Dutch painters from the 1600's, and also John Singer Sargent and Norman Rockwell. I'm also in love with Medieval paintings and prints.

I grew up in a family of porcelain doll-collecting women and only had a slight interest in dolls myself; back then I preferred Barbie. I had a curiosity in collecting special edition Barbies but tossed the idea when BJD's showed up in my life. I became an Asian ball-jointed doll fan in 2012 when affording one became a reality. They appealed to me greatly because I've always been one for customizing my own stuff and tackling hands-on projects.

Now I'm hooked on ball-jointed dolls. I think the softness indicated by the pastel on resin and the slight anime-esc facial proportions make them the perfect image of surreal human beauty. Male BJD's have my heart, and I tend to gravitate toward dolls with closer-to-natural features and those with pointy ears. As I write this, I currently have four 1/3 sized dolls and one tiny.

I joined the Youtube community and uploaded my first video of myself opening Raivo's box—my first BJD. My channel is called The Doll Scholar (formerly Maiden-TrollBlood), I make videos to help people get started with their face-ups and also talk about the hobby in general. I enjoy sewing, painting, playing video games from past decades, listening to heavy metal music, and writing.

Thank you so much for your support! And be on the lookout for future books on How to ROCK at BJD Face-Up!

Now available at most major retailers: *Make Your Own Wigs for BJD and Any Other Doll*, by Jesslyn Carver.

Works Cited

Everything I wrote about face-up was written off the top of my head based on how I do the process, but when it came to remembering certain aspects of Color Theory, I had to consult my college textbook Design Basics. Information about alternative sealants was obtained via Youtube from PocketWolf.

Lauer, David A., and Stephen Pentak. Design Basics. Boston: Thomson Wadsworth,

2008. Print.

PocketWolf. "Alternative sealants for BJD faceups." YouTube, 26 March. 2014. Web. 29

May. 2014.

CPSIA information can be obtained
at www.ICGtesting.com
Printed in the USA
LVHW071414050520
655046LV00013B/1224